MAKING
THE
RADICAL
UNIVERSITY

MAKING THE RADICAL UNIVERSITY

IDENTITY AND POLITICS

ON THE AMERICAN

COLLEGE CAMPUS,

1966–1991

ELIZABETH M. KALBFLEISCH

University of Massachusetts Press
Amherst and Boston

ISBN 978-1-62534-759-6 (paper); 760-2 (hardcover)

Designed by Sally Nichols
Set in Adobe Caslon Pro
Printed and bound by Books International, Inc.

Cover design by adam b. bohannon

Library of Congress Cataloging-in-Publication Data
Names: Kalbfleisch, Elizabeth M., author.
Title: Making the radical university : identity and politics on the
American college campus, 1966–1991 / Elizabeth M. Kalbfleisch.
Description: Amherst : University of Massachusetts Press, [2024] | Includes
bibliographical references and index.
Identifiers: LCCN 2023017489 (print) | LCCN 2023017490 (ebook) | ISBN
9781625347596 (paperback) | ISBN 9781625347602 (hardcover) | ISBN
9781685750398 (ebook)
Subjects: LCSH: Universities and colleges—Curricula—United
States—History—20th century. | Identity politics—United
States—History—20th century. | Multicultural education—United
States—History—20th century. | Canon (Literature)
Classification: LCC LB2361.5 .K35 2024 (print) | LCC LB2361.5 (ebook) |
DDC 378/.0109730904—dc23/eng/20230815
LC record available at https://lccn.loc.gov/2023017489
LC ebook record available at https://lccn.loc.gov/2023017490

British Library Cataloguing-in-Publication Data
A catalog record for this book is available from the British Library.

Furthermore:
a program of the J. M. Kaplan Fund

This work has been supported by the Furthermore: a program of the J. M. Kaplan Fund.

FOR NICK AND JONAH

CONTENTS

vii

PREFACE

This book began about fifteen years ago, in my second year of doctoral studies, when I read an article in the *New York Times* by Rachel Donadio about the so-called canon wars of the 1980s and 1990s. I was a child then, so I wasn't aware of this episode in real time. However by 2007, having spent nearly all of my adult life in academia, I had a vague notion of what the canon wars were. Donadio's article was occasioned by the thirtieth anniversary of the publication of *The Closing of the American Mind*, Allan Bloom's surprisingly popular polemic about the changes to academic curricula that had been happening since the 1960s and a key text of the canon wars. The article piqued my curiosity as something that might be worth investigating, but needing to get on with my doctoral studies in rhetoric, I filed it away for another day.

A day came in the academic year 2013–2014, my first year of a tenure-track professorship in an English department, when space unexpectedly opened up in my research agenda. At this time I returned to Donadio's article and read the various books mentioned there. What very quickly became clear was that in the canon wars lay explanations of some crises the humanities and the larger culture were facing in 2014. The academic crises manifested in seemingly endless articles about the death of the liberal arts and the humanities and the problems of English departments (that, incidentally, continue to this day). The social crises were the beginning of over a decade of racial and social unrest stemming from the vigilante murder of Trayvon Martin in 2012 and the subsequent acquittal of George Zimmerman for that murder in 2013. Additionally, 2014 saw the murder of Michael Brown and the inhuman ways his death was treated by the police force of Ferguson,

Missouri. As I was researching a different book throughout the rest of the 2010s, chaos reigned: cancel culture, the reemergence of the concept of being "woke," the emergence of Donald Trump as a Republican presidential candidate and his shocking election to that position, the increasing derangement of the Republican Party in support of the Trump presidency, hysteria over critical race theory in K–12 education, the continued murder of Black people like George Floyd and Brionna Taylor at the hands of law enforcement, and a global pandemic. Throughout, positions on the political Left and the political Right ossified, and endless editorials were written about whether we were experiencing the beginnings of a second civil war.

It was very clear that the academic and subsequent social changes that the canon wars chronicled had a lot of explanatory power for the generally oppositional perspectives the Right and Left took in this chaotic decade, and I initially wanted to write a book about that. But it became increasingly clear in my research that the story of the relationship between the canon wars and the chaos of the 2010s couldn't be well or responsibly told without a history that didn't yet exist. This book is that history. It is the history of what preceded the academic/social eruption we knew as the canon wars and some of the polarization that has torn our country asunder in the last thirty years.

In this book, I chronicle the changes that came to academic curricula from 1966 to 1991 which were deeply concerned with identity, representation, and radical Left activism. I suggest that the changes made—social recognition of and participation in society for a whole host of people that had been left out of these spaces: women, non-Whites, differently abled, homosexuals, and genderqueer individuals—were good and necessary ones. I argue that the means used to make a lot of these changes—the conflation of education and activism, the supplantation of reason by emotion, ad hominem attacks, and the embrace of the idea that everything and anything is political—might have hurt more than they helped. Ultimately, I speculate how college curricula, especially at the level of general education, might restore a unity in diversity that our country desperately needs. It is my hope that this book will help readers understand the unrecognized academic origins of some of our current cultural chaos, and with that understanding work toward a renewed national unity.

ACKNOWLEDGMENTS

Books do not come to fruition without the invaluable assistance of editors and librarians. My editor at the University of Massachusetts Press, Brian Halley, has been a tireless supporter and advocate at every step of the way. The staff of UMass Press has been similarly supportive. Two librarians at my home institution, Southern Connecticut State University, stand out. Winnie Shyam, retired, Southern Connecticut State University Libraries, found impossible-to-find materials and citations that I could not myself locate. Rebecca Hedreen, librarian and technology whiz extraordinaire, patiently fielded almost daily queries about databases not working and panic over citation managers I did not—but should have—used. Additionally, Dina Kellems, archivist at Indiana University, provided access to some materials crucial to chapter 1 and answered questions about them promptly and enthusiastically.

Equally important are supportive family and friends. Here I count as essential my husband, Nick Robinette, and my son, Jonah Kalbfleisch-Robinette, who keep me going; my parents, Mike Kalbfleisch and the late Monica Jan, and my grandparents John and Dorothy Kalbfleisch who held expectations for academic success and modeled for me curiosity and a love of reading; and my siblings, Eryn Kalbfleisch, John Kalbfleisch, James Kalbfleisch, and Zak Collins, because they are awesome. Indispensable too are the friends who tirelessly listened, problem-solved, discussed, and, when necessary, distracted me: Elizabeth Austin, associate professor of English, Central Connecticut State University; Troy Paddock, CSU Professor of History, Southern

Connecticut State University; Mary Beth Pennington, master lecturer in English at Old Dominion University; and Elena Schmitt, professor of TESOL, Southern Connecticut State University.

Finally, I would like to thank the Connecticut State Colleges and Universities system for providing more than $20,000 of research grant money in the last six years for completion of this manuscript.

MAKING
THE
RADICAL
UNIVERSITY

INTRODUCTION

O N THE MORNING OF November 9, 2016, as much of the country awoke to the devastating political news of Donald Trump's election to the U.S. presidency, a startling passage made the rounds on the internet. It was from a book written in 1998 by the late philosopher Richard Rorty, and it read,

> Many writers on socioeconomic policy have warned that the old industrialized democracies are heading into a Weimar-like period, one in which populist movements are likely to overturn constitutional governments. [Further, scholars have claimed] that members of labor unions, and unorganized, unskilled workers, will sooner or later realize that their government is not even trying to prevent wages from sinking or to prevent jobs from being exported. Around the same time, they will realize that suburban White-collar workers—themselves desperately afraid of being downsized—are not going to let themselves be taxed to provide social benefits for anyone else.
>   At that point, something will crack. The non-suburban electorate will decide that the system has failed and start looking around for a strongman to vote for—someone willing to assure them that, once he is elected, the smug bureaucrats, tricky lawyers, overpaid bond salesmen and postmodernist professors will no longer be calling the shots. . . . Once such a strongman takes office, nobody can predict what will happen. . . . One thing that is very likely to happen is that the gains made in the past forty years by Black and brown Americans, and by homosexuals, will be wiped out. Jocular contempt for women will come back into fashion. The words "nigger" and "kike" will once again be heard in the workplace. All the sadism which the *academic Left* has tried to make unacceptable to its students will come flooding back. All the resentment which badly educated Americans feel about having their manners dictated to them by college graduates will find an outlet.[1]

I

Any reader with even a cursory understanding of the forces that converged to elect Donald Trump in 2016 will see the frightening prophecy in the words above.

The academic Left that Rorty mentions here refers in part to activism by professors and students in American higher education that, beginning in the 1960s, agitated for change in what was taught in higher education and who taught it. This curricular activism sought to foster changes in American thought and structure, in the direction of a greater openness toward people who had previously been excluded: women, non-White people, the poor and working class, the differently abled, homosexuals, and nonbinary individuals. Such ends were noble, progressive, and on the right side of history. This academic curricular activism had a profoundly transformative effect on American culture. For example, the extent to which many Americans are more open to previously marginalized groups, or even the degree to which many think in terms of "identity" at this point, is due in part to an academic-activist hybrid pedagogy and scholarship that was developed by students and teachers working within this paradigm.

The university's focus on identity had an enormous effect on American culture, an effect that almost cannot be overstated. There are many things one could cite to illustrate this impact, but here I describe a few books that came out in the popular press around 2018, nearly all of them written by American university professors. All of them were in some way reflecting on the legacy of the university's then-forty-year-long concern with identity and the political apparatus that had grown up around it, commonly known as identity politics. For example, Francis Fukuyama, presently the director of a graduate program in international policy at Stanford University, wrote *Identity: The Demand for Dignity and the Politics of Resentment*. In this book Fukuyama explains that by the nineteenth century, several concepts that characterize our contemporary notion of identity were in place in Western culture, particularly "the distinction between the inner and outer selves, the valuation of the inner being above existing social arrangements, the understanding that the dignity of the inner self rests on its moral freedom, the view that all human beings share this moral freedom, and the demand that the free inner self be recognized." Of the identity politics that have arisen from this meaning of identity, however, Fukuyama sees nothing inherently wrong, but nevertheless considers them troublesome because of how "identity is interpreted or asserted in certain specific ways." He describes four. The first is the way some progressives have asserted identity in lieu of complex problem-solving around the issue of growing socioeconomic inequality since the 1980s. A second problem is that identity is often used to describe smaller and smaller groups of people at the expense of larger groups whose problems aren't getting as much attention, such as the opioid crisis among lower income Americans. The third problem Fukuyama finds is one often cited by people across the political spectrum: the way identity and identity politics seem to constrain free speech, often in detrimental ways. The final problem is that such politics give rise to both political correctness and a concurrent rise of identity politics on the Right.[2]

Similarly, Kwame Anthony Appiah, a professor of philosophy and law at New York University, wrote *The Lies That Bind: Rethinking Identity*. In this book, he describes the essences that may or may not make up many of our contemporary claims about identity. In a claim that expresses a sentiment similar to that expressed in the opening page of this book, he shows how class identities may be constructed and pitted against each other. He finds that "one strand of the populist explosion [coming from those asserting a working-class identity] that tipped Donald Trump into power was an expression of resentment [by the working class] against a class defined by its education and its values: the cosmopolitan, the degree laden people who dominate the media, the public culture and the professions in our country."[3] Here he alludes to the "coastal elites" that conservatives have tried to turn the rest of the country against since the 1980s. Mark Lilla, a professor of humanities at Columbia University wrote *The Once and Future Liberal: After Identity Politics*. This book is almost exclusively concerned with the notion of identity that arose out of higher education in the post-Vietnam era. He suggests that the academic practice of identity and politics has given rise to the "Facebook model of identity: the self as a home page I construct like a personal brand, linked to others through associations I can 'like' and 'unlike' at will." This model fosters too the "Facebook model of political engagement," which is about "the self, my *very* self, not about common histories or the common good or even ideas."[4] Several other books published around 2018 explore similar terrain.[5]

Despite this effect, curiously, the origins of academia's concern with identity and practice of identity politics have heretofore gone unchronicled. This book aims to do that. It describes the start of this curricular activism and its dispersion into the larger terrain of American culture. The first chapter, "Curricular Activism on Campus, 1966–1971," explores the idea of a "new radical" as theorized by Christopher Lasch in the early 1960s as a new American "type" developing out of the Progressive era. This new radical was primarily focused on cultural criticism; furthermore, they engaged in these activities as their paid labor. The chapter then moves into a reading of several primary documents from the well-studied Students for a Democratic Society (SDS), which identified the university as an ideal site for the activist energies of the new radical; it examines SDS's well known Port Huron Statement in addition to the less-well-known Radical Education Project. It also examines the development of the New University Conference, a short-lived annual meeting for student and faculty radicals who sought to establish the university as a site of disruption and activism. The chapter then turns to examining the activist efforts of faculty, focusing on pedagogy and scholarship. Finally, the chapter reviews the development of the first "minority studies" disciplines: Black studies, ethnic studies, and women's studies.

Chapter 2, "Identity, Politics, and Identity Politics," traces the origins of academia's focus on identity and the development of an academic notion of politics, two phenomena that merged and came to be known as identity politics. It first discusses the notion of identity as theorized by psychologist Erik Erikson in the 1950s. Then it turns to examining a distinctly academic notion of the political that suggests "politics" refers to understanding the ways cultural artifacts may illuminate unequal power relations between people, and that such illumination will somehow ameliorate inequality. It briefly explores how this academic notion of the political is apparent in critical theory, a new paradigm for work in the humanities and social sciences that was also developing in the post-Vietnam era. Finally, the bulk of the chapter is devoted to reading the original texts of identity politics. This reading explores the claims, beliefs, and positions expressed in these texts to describe the intellectual character of the origins of identity politics.

The third chapter, "The Canon Wars and Identity Politics at Stanford," examines a high-profile national debate over the general education curriculum at Stanford University in 1986–1988, one of the most recognized episodes of the "canon wars" of the 1980s. It traces the conflict back to a general education revision in the late 1970s at Stanford that was in line with national concerns and arguments about what general education was for and what it should look like, a conversation in which many elite institutions were engaged in the 1970s. Such changes included the development of race, class, and gender as an interpretive paradigm for general undergraduate academic work, a paradigm that can be understood as the ideology of identity politics condensed and packaged into a somewhat tidy entity for undergraduate pedagogy. This cultural conversation evolved into the canon wars of the 1980s, and this chapter argues that these disputes should be understood as an example of a national audience becoming aware of the activities of the curricular activism of the previous two decades, as opposed to just another battle between conservatives and liberals in an ongoing culture war.

Chapter 4, "The Escalating Canon Wars and Racism and Sexism at the University of Texas, Austin," opens up with a brief discussion of the other highly influential controversy of the late 1980s canon wars—Allan Bloom's *The Closing of the American Mind*. From there it further discusses those disputes and shows how they evolved, as the 1980s became the 1990s, into an explosion of articles and books in the scholarly and popular press on political correctness, multiculturalism, illiberalism, and the radicalism that had been developing in academia since the 1960s. It then turns to another curricular battle over the undergraduate curriculum, this time at the University of Texas, Austin (UT Austin). Here the controversy raged over just one class, rather than over an entire general education curriculum, as it had at Stanford—Rhetoric 306, a written composition class required of nearly all UT Austin's undergraduates. At issue was a revision to the class meant to make it more uniform across the hundreds of sections offered each semester. A committee proposed making the class about "diversity" and using a controversial sociology textbook,

Paula S. Rothenberg's *Racism and Sexism: An Integrated Study* as the uniform text across sections. The chapter examines the various support for and objections to such a change and shows that the revision was entirely abandoned altogether after the committee working on it felt they did not have the support of their administration, whom they believed had caved to pressure by outside forces arising from the national attention the change had garnered. The chapter closes by discussing the focus of the canon wars moving on to a concern about multiculturalism in the early 1990s.

Finally, in the conclusion, I praise the ends of the academic Left's activism while exploring some of the collateral damage of the means by which they achieved their ends. I argue that the means used have contributed to the political polarization that we live with today and discuss one way that a renewed look at establishing common general education programs may heal some of this polarization.

This book seeks to tell an origin story, as it were, of identity politics and the paradigm of race, class, and gender that academics have been working with for nearly half a century now. Consequently, it does not explore two closely related developments of this era—critical race theory and disability studies. The origins of disability studies as an academic field is often dated to 1984 with Anne M. Donnellan's article "The Criterion of the Least Dangerous Assumption."[6] Critical race theory as an academic field of study did not have wide recognition before the 1990s.[7] These very important developments could be seen as a sort of "volume 2" of the developments chronicled in this manuscript, and accordingly are not addressed here.

The ends sought by these academic activists were fundamentally transformative and undoubtedly beneficial to American culture. The means by which they achieved these ends created some perhaps unrecognized collateral damage that needs to be recognized and reconciled. I hope to make a clear case for both.

CHAPTER I

CURRICULAR ACTIVISM ON CAMPUS, 1966-1971

THERE IS A LONGSTANDING belief on the part of the American Left, both progressive and radical, that educational policies and institutions are ideal sites for achieving social change. Since the early twentieth century, those who wanted to change the cultural, political, and/or social conditions of the United States from the Left have set their sights on education. For example, as is well known, the early twentieth-century progressives strongly influenced American K–12 public schooling. Although there were certainly radical strains in early twentieth-century progressivism, mostly these groups were interested in bringing change via reform of existing circumstances.

The reform efforts of early twentieth-century progressive educational activists were aimed at creating Americans who were collectively minded to help the functioning of American industry, rather than individually driven, as so many seemed to be. Progressives, having different ideas about how to implement educational reform, shared a commitment to an idea that the future would require an organized and cooperative society where everyone had their specialist roles to perform. Further, this social vision meant that people's beliefs and values needed to change. "Rugged and independent individualism" had to be discouraged in the interest of teaching people to be cooperative and to some extent collective. Consequently, these progressive educational theories went beyond imparting facts and skills. They recognized that to achieve their aims, they needed to work on the very character and psychological outlook of the Americans they hoped to mold: "The first goal of the educators and the social

7

reformers who adopted this vision of the well-ordered society was to change the basis of human motivation from desire for economic gain to unselfish interest in working for the good of society."[1]

As it happened, out of this progressivism developed a strain of radicalism that was particularly suited to creating belief systems that might be promoted through educational channels.[2] Dubbed the "new radicals," these individuals constituted a new "class" in society, the intellectuals, who were defined "broadly, as a person for whom thinking fulfills at once the function of work and play; more specifically, as a person whose relationship to society is defined, both in his eyes and in the eyes of society, principally by his presumed capacity to comment upon it with greater detachment then those more directly caught up in the practical business of production and power."[3] These early century radicals sought to upend various social institutions: the middle-class family, relations between the sexes, and a capitalist mode of economic life. Thus, the groundwork for activism on college campuses, especially regarding the beliefs and values Americans held, was laid several decades earlier than the 1960s, at the dawn of the development mass education in America.

Further, postwar America brought many changes to politics and culture that also helped create conditions conducive to the campus activism that arose in the 1960s. There was rampant talk in the 1950s about the "post-industrial" society and the "affluent society." Such social conditions were created in part by the "old" American Left (in contrast to the "new" Left, made up of student radicals, discussed subsequently in this chapter), which helped foster a "discourse of abundance" that created space to develop "postmaterialist" or "post-economic" thinking in American intellectual life. These two other ways of describing the post-industrial society were "a boon to creative and critical thinking in the 1960s." The university was quite important to this new social structure. For one, bureaucratic social relations such as those created by corporations, the military, and universities became important to the social needs of the post-industrial society. Additionally, from the late 1950s to the late 1960s there was an increase in "the institutions and media involved in the pursuit of knowledge and the cultivation of sensibility. Higher education became a broad-based, organized social resource, available to large numbers of young people on a more democratic basis than ever before and became closely integrated with both public agencies and organized private interests outside the academy."[4] Indeed, the sheer number of students attending college exploded after World War II with attendance doubling in the decade of 1960–1970. Additionally, the intelligentsia thought that professors "held the key to the political future of the post industrial society."[5]

So it happened, then, that the social conditions facing students entering college in the 1960s were vastly different than even a decade before. Children born in the 1940s before and after World War II grew up in a society becoming post-industrial and affluent to a degree previously unknown. They developed into the student activists of the 1960s who have received so much historical attention (though they were really only a small percentage of college students) and who were centrally concerned with radical Leftist politics—the "new" Left—and believed themselves to constitute a class of "new radicals." Although many of them would eventually become new radicals of the intellectual type that Christopher Lasch chronicled, these activists in the 1960s were first of all young, American students on college campuses; however, they were also self-consciously international, drawing a connection to dissident activity practiced by young people all over the world. Their agenda was political, but not only—it was also a "search for a psychic community in which one's identity can be defined, social and personal relationships based on love can be established and can grow, unfettered by the cramping pressures of the careers and life styles so characteristic of America today."[6] These student activists were also captivated by an existential alienation that resulted in a common criticism of "dissociation." This dissociation appeared in debates throughout the 1960s, and it connoted a "disabling, demoralizing, distance between self and others, between actions and consequences."[7] Then, too, politically, these new young radicals violently rejected liberalism, seeing it as an "enemy" on par with totalitarianism and authoritarianism. Student activists thought that education was an integral part of their activism because colleges and universities were the places where many of them were encountering the radicalism they came to embrace.

Both of these definitions of the new radicalism—Lasch's and the student activists'—in the early 1960s pointed toward an aspect of the Leftist radical agenda stretching back decades: the radical reformation of American education, specifically in the direction of inculcating *belief* in something. Early twentieth-century radicals focused their educational energies on primary, secondary, and worker education; midcentury student Left radicals set their sights on American higher education. Disillusioned at an early age by vast contradictions between the discourse and ideals of the affluent society and the lived reality of Black peoples' interminable marginalization and brutalization, the apathy of mass society, and the constant threat of nuclear annihilation, the students participating in the campus movements of the 1960s set out to remake America so that it might more closely resemble the ideal it espoused. One student activist group that has received much attention in the histories of this era, Students for a Democratic Society (SDS), first set out their philosophy in 1962 in an oft-evolving document known as the Port Huron Statement (PHS). SDS was a powerful student group that began as the "organizational center" of a number of student activists at Harvard that called themselves the "new Left." At their most powerful in 1969, they had a "hundred thousand members, hundreds of chapters, [and] millions of supporters."[8] The PHS was a manifesto of sorts that expressed doubt that the mainstream Republican and Democratic political parties could achieve the kind and degree of transformation that SDS believed necessary. Therefore, they identified the universities as "an overlooked seat of influence" that might allow them to achieve their desired radical transformation. SDS turned to the university because it held "a permanent position of social influence" that "[made] it a crucial institution in the formation of social attitudes." SDS further noted that those in power heavily relied on the knowledge produced by the universities and that the university was useful for SDS's agenda because it was open to such a diversity of viewpoints, meaning that even a radically transformative worldview like the SDS's might be tolerable. The PHS treated the above points as facts about American universities, true, "no matter how dull the teaching, how paternalistic the rules, how irrelevant the research that goes on. Social relevance, the accessibility to knowledge, and internal openness—these together make the university a potential base and agency in a movement of social change." The statement then offers a mini-manifesto for the idea of the university as a site of Leftist/socialist social change. It states,

1. Any new Left in America must be, in large measure, a Left with real intellectual skills, committed to deliberativeness, honesty, reflection as working tools. The university permits the political life to be an adjunct to the academic one and action informed by reason.

2. A new Left must be distributed in significant social roles throughout the country. The universities are distributed in such a manner.

3. A new Left must consist of younger people who matured in the post-war world, and partially be directed to the recruitment of younger people. The university is an obvious beginning point.

4. A new Left must include liberals and socialists, the former for their relevance, the latter for their sense of thoroughgoing reforms in the system. The university is a more sensible place than a political party for these two traditions to begin to discuss their differences and look for political synthesis.

5. A new Left must start controversy across the land, if national policies and national apathy are to be reversed. The ideal university is a community of controversy within itself and its effects on communities beyond.

6. A new Left must transform modern complexity into issues that can be understood and felt close up by every human being. It must give form to the feelings of helplessness and indifference, so that people may see the political, social, and economic sources of their private troubles and organize to change society. In a time of supposed prosperity, moral complacency, and political manipulation, a new Left cannot rely on only aching stomachs to be the engine force of social reform. The case for change, for alternatives that will involve uncomfortable personal efforts, must be argued as never before. The university is a relevant place for all of these activities.

SDS recognized that the university could not alone achieve all these goals. Instead, a "university reform[ed] by an alliance of students and faculty" was the appropriate site for a "militant Left" to "awaken" allies who could, in partnership with university stakeholders, achieve the social revolution outlined here.[9]

SDS's educational aspirations, as outlined in the PHS, have a tenuous Marxist affiliation, which would grow and intensify in the following years. In the early 1960s, when the PHS was drafted, the student radicals were careful to avoid an alliance with Marxism, especially as they were trying to shed the "baggage" of the old American Left that had grown weak and disillusioned in the 1950s from, among other things, McCarthyism. The student radicals who composed the PHS did not want to be taken as doctrinaire communists but nor were they as rabidly anticommunist as some of their elders, the disillusioned old Left. Criticism they received from this old Left ironically made the early SDS somewhat more open to communism than they might have otherwise been.[10] Thus, in the middle of the decade, as SDS experienced rapid growth, Marxism influenced SDS by providing an intellectual structure to their movement, which had otherwise been theoretically inchoate. The young people that made up the new Left believed that the old Marxism of the Russian Revolution could not explain the distinctly American radicalism that was evident in Black political activism of the 1940s and 1950s that came to fruition in the civil rights movement. Further, as historian Paul Buhle claimed, "Inasmuch as the working class neither appeared within reach of emancipating itself nor demonstrated any interest in Marxist doctrine, the presence of rampant injustice and of desires for drastic change induced a sense of despair (especially when racial efforts lagged) and a thirst for knowledge that might someday be useful." Thus, there was a feeling of the need to "start over," intellectually, among the student radicals of the 1960s. The new Marxism that the student radicals sought came via Herbert Marcuse's *Eros and Civilization*, an attempted synthesis of Freudian and Marxist theory. Marcuse was a member of the Frankfurt school of social critics and his text, along with Theodor Adorno and Max Horkheimer's *Dialectic of the Enlightenment*, was the intellectual backbone of the student movement seeking a new Marxism to guide their activism.[11]

In 1966, four years after the distribution of the PHS, SDS made one of the first concerted attempts to radicalize the university along the line of ideas outlined in the statement. This effort is described in a document called the Radical Education Project (REP), which was meant to be "an independent educational, research and publication program initiated by Students for a Democratic Society, dedicated to the cause of a democratic radicalism, and aspiring to the creation of a new Left in America." The REP, among other things, sought to develop a "radical (or utopian) ideology" that stood in opposi-tional distinction to "American (status quo) ideology," defined as "the adjustment of the myths of the 'American way of life'—free enter-prise, individualism, progress, pluralism, pragmatism, etc.—to the particular social conditions of people in different social locations." As the document states, "One aim of the Radical Education Project is to assist the [student] movement in better understanding American ideology and to develop more clearly and effectively radical ideol-ogy." The REP document outlines an extensive program for how this radical ideology would be developed. It recommends the creation of study groups to produce a wide range of relevant knowledge about human beings and their existence in various parts of a world domi-nated by the Western military-industrial complex. The knowledge to be developed falls into four categories: (1) "values and utopia," (2) "myths and reality," (3) "strategies of change," and (4) "programs toward new constituencies." The Radical Education Project docu-ment echoes the focus on the university as a site of change described in the PHS by naming the university as a "potential agent of change." The REP authors state an expectation that "most SDS members and many of its 'non student' supporters are university based. And many of the student members will be in universities once they finish their intellectual and radical apprenticeship."[12] It is unclear if by this last statement, the authors of the REP believed that SDS members would continue their activism in universities or if they thought these activ-ists would be in universities later as faculty members. In either case, it is clear that the REP maintained the central focus of SDS on the universities as the established institutional site from which to launch their makeover of American society, a makeover that in its emphasis on "false consciousness" and "political economy," among other things, revealed a growing allegiance to Marxism.

   The REP outlines a set of strategies for creating new "constituen-cies" sympathetic to their program of bringing people out of the false consciousness regarding the American myths they lived by. Partially, this involved the creation of a task force to "begin [a] reconstruction of intellectual theory and teaching [by developing] radical educational materials for students in introductory liberal arts courses." More specifically, the REP seeks the development of

> a thinking man's guide—a radical critique and reformulation of the discipline geared to the introductory textbooks that students are required to use . . . ; supplementary reading material and annotated bibliography; guides for the organization of "counter courses"; question and answer sequences—"scenarios"—to force the instructor and class to deal with relevant issues and to expose the value biases of the "accepted truth." These materials would be made available to SDS and other students through the local chapter and sympathetic faculty, and, hopefully also through sale at the local bookstores as a supplement to the required texts.[13]

Initially, four disciplines of introductory liberal arts courses were identified as sites where this educational effort should be aimed: economics, political science, sociology, and history. The REP document further expresses interest in developing radical supplemental materials for philosophy, psychology, anthropology, and literary criticism shortly thereafter.

The SDS group that developed the REP did not limit their concerns to undergraduate students in the liberal arts; they were equally concerned with radicalizing professional education. The REP document suggests that the university trained professionals that "give poor service" and were generally conservative and adherent to a status quo. Further, the SDS REP group expressed a concern that "too often, it seems that the idea of profession [*sic*] as a means to social status and mobility has replaced the ideal of a profession as a means of public service." The REP recognized that many of the students agitating for change on campus would themselves soon be professionals in a variety of areas. Thus, the writers of the REP recognized that radically overhauling education would be a way to overhaul professional practice in a variety of areas in a few years, when the radical student would have less time for activism because they would be working professionals. Accordingly, the REP's focus on professional education required teaching professionals to overcome "the tendency of the society to

isolate and transform the individual before he can organize and transform the society." Thus, the REP "project on the professions" would

> organize groups of radicals in, or preparing for, professions. It will
> assist these groups in preparing and disseminating educational
> materials dealing with: the structure of the profession; the dominant
> values of the profession; its links with and relation to the status quo;
> the treatment of dissidents in the profession; the range and limits of
> freedom; the nature and a critique of the nature of professional educa-
> tion; a manifesto of values and professional responsibility; a program
> describing the institutional and technique changes needed to be in the
> profession; and a guide to opportunities and ways of operating in the
> profession which contribute to the social change ideals of democratic
> radicalism.[14]

The next year, SDS showed they had made good on these intentions to radicalize the professions. In October 1967, the Radical Education Project published *Radicals in the Professions*, the proceedings
of a conference of the same name held that summer. The introduction recognizes, as did the REP manifesto of 1966, that most radicals
would take up positions in the professions once their student days
had ended, though they would inevitably encounter problems like
maintaining their radicalism.[15]

The conference proceedings note that approximately 250 professionals from journalism; social work; city planning; law; the ministry;
primary, secondary, and higher education; and healthcare attended.
The document also outlines foundational ways the radical professional would act out their radical status: (1) behaving as an organizer
by "focusing attention on problems, and by calling into question the
accepted practices and traditions of his profession and of the community"; (2) serving as an educator who "[connects] social, political,
and economic issues [and thereby forces] people to ask fundamental questions about society."[16] The selected papers included in the
volume of proceedings discuss what this radical professional stance
might look like in city planning, medicine, "ghetto" schools, and law.

In the spring of 1968, following the conference, Tom Hayden,
Noam Chomsky, and other radicals organized another conference
in Chicago that represented the most direct and concerted effort to
radicalize the university: the New University Conference (NUC).

The NUC was not a conference per se but rather a movement poised to fundamentally disrupt and break down the American university system. The NUC was an "alliance of radical graduate students and professors largely unknown outside the academic and New Left communities."[17] By August 1968, the organization had put out its second newsletter, which stated that the organization had grown rapidly from March to August and that its main goal was to organize the radical academics who had otherwise been working in isolation, away from one another. The newsletter's authors hoped that the NUC would provide "a stable group for discussion, strategic thinking, political clarification, and concerted action." The newsletter echoed the concerns expressed in both the REP document and the "Radicals in the Professions" conference about providing moral support for the radical professional academic, as well as a sort of jealous admiration of the organized student movement.[18]

The organization had better than 100 percent growth between 1970 and 1971, going from four hundred to more than eight hundred members and twenty to forty-one chapters. The organization disrupted the 1970 meetings of the American Association for the Advancement of Science, the American Historical Association, and the Modern Language Association. The NUC's goal in such activities was to organize "educational workers at their workplace" and develop a "working class consciousness among academicians." The NUC campus organizer was charged with "[creating] conflict between school authorities and faculty or students; between boards of education and communities; between corporate criminals and victims. For he knows that only in a conflict situation do issues become clear, does liberal rhetoric lie exposed, and does the mobilization of a powerful movement become possible." The NUC developed Open Up Our Schools, or OUTS, as the central strategy for "disrupt[ing] and eventually destroy[ing] the university system as presently conceived," notably their ties to the capitalist systems and service of the "ruling class." These OUTS schools would provide "various kinds of Workers, socializing people into their expected roles, maintaining various positions within the working class, 'cooling out' the aspirations of third World, poor White, and Women students." The hope was that these activist schools would ensure the failure of the capitalist system.

Further, members expected that OUTS would serve as a homebase, as it were, for a "sustained, revolutionary movement in the schools."[19] For all the sound and fury displayed by the organization in 1971, though, the organization did not last. By 1972, the organization was bankrupt and voted to disband. In spite of what may look like a crash landing, however, in a short period of time, scholars have claimed that the NUC left a "startling" legacy apparent in "campus-based child care centers, graduate assistant unions, and radical professional caucuses. . . . It introduced ideas of radical education to many campuses and was active in the movement against the Vietnam war."[20]

Although the energies and organization of the students were impressive on their own, it is doubtful the movement would have seen such success without sympathetic elders. The protest efforts that characterized campus life in the 1960s—and were the major vehicle of campus radicalism—had always been a union of faculty and students. Faculty, however, often focused their radical Left political energies on the curriculum, their main area of expertise. The impact of radical faculty in seeking to reform the university and of a mind with the goals of the REP was evident in, for example, a book series first published by Random House in 1968, Pantheon Anti-Textbooks. This series is a set of edited collections of essays on the university as a whole and on individual disciplines, collecting the work of "young scholars and the criticisms which they have to offer both of the way in which their subject is being taught and of the role that it is playing in the society as a whole."[21] The inaugural collection, *The Dissenting Academy: Essays Criticizing the Teaching of the Humanities in American Universities*, brought together scholars of English, economics, history, international relations, anthropology, and philosophy to answer the question: "Does the business-as-usual of the American academic community do more to assist in the production of Vietnams than it does to examine, resist, and correct policy that lead to such moral disaster?"[22] Generally, the scholars collected in this work displayed a firm resistance to American involvement in the Vietnam War, though they were substantially more measured in their criticisms than the student radicals, as befitted their more mature status. Mostly, the essays exhibit a frustration with the academy for evolving into an arm of the military-industrial complex rather than realizing the academy's nineteenth- and early twentieth-century aspirations to produce useful knowledge that responds to common and visible problems of humanity.

The editor of the volume, Theodore Roszak, contributed an essay that examined the failure of humanistic and social science scholars to do work that is relevant, meaningful to a larger community outside the academy, and that addresses social problems. He believed that the way academics were trained—in disciplines that require fealty on local and national levels—had created this scholarly disengagement, which he considered the abdication of the moral and civic function of the scholar. Rather, he wanted scholars in the humanities and social sciences to model themselves on the *philosophes* of the Enlightenment, practitioners of a "socially aggressive inquisitiveness" that characterized their intellectual endeavors.[23] Louis Kampf, a humanities professor at MIT, contributed an essay titled "The Scandal of Literary Scholarship." The details of scandal are three: the lack of, or lacking quality of, standards of literary scholarship; the fact that too much literary scholarship is produced; and the fact that what is produced is ignorant of social concerns. Kampf was critical of the way in which professional activity in English was not really about literature—it was about advancing throughout the profession and gaining accolades. His solution to this titular scandal was to turn to Karl Marx's work as an aid in literary interpretation and to conceive of literature as a tool for "agitation."[24]

Sumner M. Rosen, an economist working in and out of academia who had served as an advisor to SDS, wrote an essay that dissented from mainstream economics by suggesting some challenges to the Keynesian orthodoxy then dominant in most economics programs.[25] Staughton Lynd, the historian of the group and an avowed Marxian socialist, contributed an essay on the uses and duties of the dissident historian. Lynd directed historians to examine history for insight into how people should live, rather than for an account of "how things really happened," which Lynd suggested was the dominant model of historiography in the 1960s.[26] Marshall Windmiller, a political scientist, decried how scholars in international relations used the cover of "expertise" to avoid criticizing the Johnson administration.[27] Some but not all of these faculty scholars explicitly embraced a Marxist paradigm for the revolutionary work they were trying to do, echoing a dominant concern of the student radicals. What all the essays in this volume have in common, though, was a strong urge to move humanities and social science scholarship toward work useful in the "real world." Most of the essayists believed that this "real world" was meant to be the focus of scholarship in a university so shaped by the Enlightenment; accordingly, there is an unmistakable postlapsarian tone to their plaints.

This idea that the humanities themselves were somehow in revolt, infected with a radical, disruptive spirit that sought to completely upend the university, persisted. An esteemed group of scholars spent 1969–1970 pondering the idea of a revolution in the humanities, and their work is collected in the volume *Liberations: New Essays on the Humanities in Revolution*, edited by Ihab Hassan, an English professor at the University of Wisconsin, Milwaukee, who was temporarily directing the Wesleyan Center for the Humanities at the time.[28] The radical energies evident in this volume concern not the "college administrator and campus guard, [the curriculum], [or] scholarship itself" but at an older, humanistic idea of man. Finding himself, and the age, disenchanted with Leonardo's Vitruvian Man, Hassan sees a post-humanism "in the making."[29] One instance of this post-humanism as described by the writer Daniel Stern was the confrontation of the horror, destruction, and alienation of the early twentieth century with novelistic explorations of "a sense of the mysterious possibilities in the body or the will—against the body or the will—against an increasingly totalitarian life—and the relationship of these possibilities to the religious sense." The motivation here was to recover the body that had been traditionally rejected in the mind-body dualism which has characterized Western philosophy. Stern named the novelists working in such a vein "postmodern" novelists. These postmodern writers treat "the body as if it were as much of a mystery as the unseen spirit."[30]

Michael Wolff, a professor of English and a major figure in Victorian Studies, argued that the humanities were currently, and rightfully, in revolution because of two central developments in the history of humanity that came out of the French and Industrial Revolutions: "first, that all human beings are equal and should so treat each other; and second, that there is no meaningful limit to the material resources available for human use." These developments led to the unsettling of a fixed social order; previously, humans did not live in societies where there was a prominent belief that things could be changed, Wolff argued. These revolutions of modernity changed that order and led to "a society [British] that had thought of itself as dependent on an order provided by King, Church, and Country [beginning] to be conscious of living under the shadow of some sort of catastrophe, often quite precisely defined as economic disaster or political upheaval." The humanities, traditionally conceived, according to Wolff, had been aimed at teaching people how to tolerate the suffering of an unchanging world. The form in which these achievements were passed down was the tradition, yet another manifestation of an order that had broken down in late modernity. The new humanities, then, that Wolff called for, "must try to see events and persons, even great ones, not in relation to traditions and heritages but to the incomplete humanity of large numbers of human beings."[31]

Hayden White's contribution to this collection, "The Culture of Criticism," suggests the humanities are in revolution because avant-garde artists like James Joyce, W. B. Yeats, Alain Robbe-Grillet, John Cage, Merce Cunningham, and Samuel Beckett had rejected the hierarchical emphasis in traditional Western conceptions of artistic and scientific form, as exemplified by Karl Popper, Erich Auerbach, and E. H. Gombrich. Instead, these artists reached toward a paratactic form that "demands a change in consciousness that will finally make a unified humanity possible."[32] White argued that avant-garde artists were providing a fundamentally new sensory and linguistic way to experience the world, which was so necessary because realism as an artistic style had long since failed to capture the experience of modernity. This notion that at the turn of the 1970s, the humanities were captured by a radical, revolutionary spirit in search of a fundamentally new way of communicating is also evident in Richard Poirier's contribution to this volume. Poirier offered an essay, "Rock of Ages," critical of the idea that there was a generation gap or that anything the young radicals of the 1960s was experiencing was new or unique at all. He suggested that "the gap between the generations is more apparent than real, that it is a metaphor in which nearly everyone has taken shelter, and that the real gap is between, on the one side, new dispositions of human power, both demographic and psychic, new forms of energy, and, on the other, the inadequacy of our customary ways of seeing, listening, and interpreting." These inadequate sensory functions were created, in part, by electronics and the revolution in communication; these developments had "changed the nature of communication and therefore the nature of social intercourse of history and politics."[33]

Thus, at the beginning of 1970, the Leftist revolutionary spirit of the 1960s (having been soundly defeated in the sphere of electoral politics, with Richard Nixon then at the beginning of his second year in office) had migrated into the university generally, the humanities specifically, and more specifically still English departments. For example, the March 1970 issue of *College English*—along with *PMLA*, the flagship scholarly journal of English studies—was a collection of papers delivered at the Modern Language Association conference in the fall of 1969. These essays reveal that English professors were expressing many of the same concerns as radical students and faculty. James E. Miller Jr., the president of the National Council of Teachers of English in 1969 and an English professor at the University of Chicago, spoke on "Classic American Writers and Radicalized Curriculum." In the essay based on this presentation, Miller wrote, "We are living in a time of crisis in which we must lay aside the old ways that have not worked and find the new ways that do work, the new visions that speak to our anguish. If we take this to heart, in our own field of American Literature, I believe that there is much that we have taught that we might now cease to teach and there is much that we have not taught that we should now teach."[34] Miller called for the inclusion of Black authors like Jean Toomer and Ralph Ellison and new novels like *Catch-22* and *One Flew Over the Cuckoo's Nest*. This author sought to challenge the American "canon"—nine American writers established by the MLA in 1956: Ralph Waldo Emerson, Henry David Thoreau, Walt Whitman, Edgar Allan Poe, Herman Melville, Nathaniel Hawthorne, Mark Twain, Henry James, and Emily Dickinson. Miller wanted to discard the works of these authors "usually" taught and look to their radical works and teach those instead.

Alan Purves, in the essay "Life, Death, and the Humanities," described a problem that "infects" the "humanities spirit" and the teaching of English, art, music, and history. The problems were (1) expertise, specialization, and disciplinarity in response to the vast explosion in information—"data"—at the end of the 1960s; (2) a celebration of technology, seemingly for technology's sake without attention to what "technology" might be properly used for; (3) disinterested students; and (4) a failure of imagination, basically to empathize with someone or something else. Purves argued that "the humanities programs that we have, and perhaps even the structure of the humanities as it exists in such a discipline as English, are monolithic acronyms that serve only to defeat the purposes that were set for them. . . . Their business is too often with death, not life." He set out foci for a reformed English/humanities. One emphasis was to "examine the ways by which our symbol systems manipulate us and the ways by which we manipulate them." He suggested, "We must take as the content of the humanities, then, not only literature, the fine arts, and music, but television, film, and shopping centers—all of what McLuhan terms the extensions of Man—because those extensions have a symbolic function and so can be considered instruments to perpetuate or destroy life." He also called for a curriculum in "symbol systems, aesthetics, and structures" and suggested he would give up both the terms "English" and "the humanities" as being too narrow and mired in the past. This curriculum must be articulated "in terms of human behavior."[35]

Perhaps the most radical essay in the collection was authored by Bruce Franklin, a scholar infamously fired by Stanford University for his campus political activity (but hired very shortly thereafter as a full professor with tenure at Rutgers University, where he remained for his career). In "The Teaching of Literature in the Highest Academies of the Empire," Franklin described university professors at a place like Stanford and characterized them as what would later be called members of the coastal liberal elite. The essay is a scathing indictment of the "scholar-critic-professor of literature": "This ignorant self-deceived parasite, perfect butt of the satire he so admires does indeed have an important role in the twilight hour of the dictatorship of the bourgeoisie." He then went on to mock the "values" these professors were supposed to teach—that of great literature at the expense of social and political action. Franklin's goal in making such strong condemnations was for the literary profession to "remold our ideas so we can join the people and serve them." Franklin condemned his faculty mentors at Stanford for not being "concerned with the major ideological questions of our century. Not one was familiar with the major ideas that attacked their own beliefs. They were universally ignorant of Marx, Engels, Lenin, Mao, and Marxist criticism."[36] The radicalism in this volume of *College English* ranges from mild to insurrectionary, as Franklin's tone indicates.

The designs on upending the academy in the late 1960s, so far explored, were perpetuated by heteronormative White men almost exclusively. Of course, those not falling into that demographic group—women, non-White people, homosexuals—were also at this time collectively giving voice to the soul-deforming prejudices inherent in American culture and history. Such *cris de coeur* began in attempts to carve out academic spaces from which to launch critiques that would deliver these marginalized peoples into the larger, complicated narrative of American life. Accordingly, the last few years of the 1960s saw the first minority studies programs develop at colleges and universities, called in the late 1960s women's studies, "ethnic" studies, and Black studies. Black studies as a distinct program was founded in 1968 at San Francisco State University after years of activism by a Black studies movement on the campus of historically Black colleges and universities and at traditionally White institutions. The hiring of Nathan Hare, a sociologist formerly of Howard University, at San Francisco State University (SFSU) marked the institutionalization of Black studies. Hare outlined the theory and practice behind a Black studies curriculum in the autumn 1969 issue of the *Massachusetts Review*, shortly before he left SFSU to, among other things, nurture his new journal, *The Black Scholar*.[37] Hare conceived of a program that had two phases—expressive and pragmatic. The "expressive" phase would have courses on Black history, arts, and culture, courses that were meant to "build in Black youth a sense of pride or self, of collective destiny, a sense of pastness as a springboard in the quest for a new and better future." Such a curriculum was also meant to "deracicize White students." The pragmatic phase dealt with giving students knowledge and skills to "deal with their society." This phase, according to Hare, was "highly functional" and would involve "courses producing socioeconomic skills (Black politics, Black economics, Black science, Black communications and so forth), extensive field work, and community involvement in collaboration with classroom activities." Hare further illustrated these remarks with course descriptions from such classes already on the books in the Black Studies Program at SFSU. For example, "Black History" (Black Studies 101) taught "African cultures from the Iron Age to the present; European colonization, contemporary nationalism; Black cultural and scientific contributions, African and American. Political, economic, and social aspects of slavery and the contemporary Black movement." "Black Math" (Black Studies 102) focused on "presentation of mathematics as a way of thinking, a means of communication and an instrument of problem solving, with special reference to the Black community, using references from Black experiences where possible for illustrative and reading-problem material. Deductive, inductive, and heuristic methods of mathematics are developed and used with special attention to application to the Black community's needs." Similarly, "Black Science" (Black Studies 104) would examine an "introduction to scientific development stressing the contributions of Black scientists. Emphasis on the application of fundamental concepts and methods of science to the environment of Black Americans."[38]

The *Massachusetts Review* staff raised questions about such a curriculum, particularly regarding implementation: "Should the aim of every Black Studies program be to serve and transform the Black community? If so, how is that aim best achieved . . . changing the usual degree or credential requirements, 'beefing up' or ignoring traditional notions of academic soundness in Black studies courses?" Hare responded,

> The notion that "academic soundness" would suffer is basically a racist apprehension, a feeling that any deviation on the part of Blacks away from White norms and standards would inevitably dip downward. It is also based, perhaps, on the naïve notion that traditional education is value free and, because it is based on the ideology of the existing political forces, is blessed with the "end of ideology." That is, most emphatically, not the case. The whole need for Black studies grows out of true academic soundness in the educational system as we know it now. A key test of soundness for any structure is whether or not it works.

Obviously our current educational system does not work for a growing number of Black and oppressed "minorities" whose backgrounds have not coincided with those of White suburbia.

When asked about whether Black studies was necessarily separatist, for Black students only, Hare replied,

Black studies is based ideally on the ideology of revolutionary nationalism; it is not based on any form of racism, Black or White, though it is dedicated, of course, to the destruction of White racism. Which may be why the establishment seems so determined . . . to confuse Black students into a search for tangential, ultra-separatist goals such as separate dormitories, chitterlings in the cafeteria and similar divisions having little to do with changing seriously the power relations of Blacks and Whites, let alone the nature of education.

Hare continued, "Black studies is nationalist, not separatist. . . . Revolutionary nationalism . . . seeks to transfer power, at least a portion thereof, to an oppressed group, and in that effort is more tolerant of White radicals."[39]

At the same time in the late 1960s and early 1970s, academic activists made calls for ethnic studies, a curricular reform related but not identical to Black studies. In the summer of 1969, in a special issue of the interdisciplinary journal *Soundings* titled "Toward a New University," an economics professor at Western Washington State College, Thad H. Spratlen, defined "ethnic" as emphasizing "the life experience, traits, conditions, and behavior of non-White minorities in the United States. Primary reference is to Blacks or Afro-Americans, American Indians, Puerto Ricans, Mexican Americans, and other such groups of African, Indian, or Spanish descent." He suggested that these groups needed special attention in a college curriculum because

These are the people for whom the promise of America has been denied or betrayed to such a degree that their way of life and their place in the society differ greatly from that of most White Americans. A basic premise of the discussion [concerning ethnic studies programs] is that as we become aware of their distinctiveness (ethnicity), we also become aware of the omissions, distortions, and misunderstandings that are characteristic of traditional White, middle-class American and European-oriented educational programs, practices and policies.

If corrections are to be made, a fundamental reorientation in curricular programs will be required.[40]

In this article, Spratlen outlined the goals that an ethnic studies program might achieve:

1. To stimulate inquiry into and understanding of minority groups and the contributions which their members have made and continue to make, to the totality of American life;

2. To enable students to develop comprehensive and balanced perspectives on the realities and experiences of both White and non-White life in a White-dominated society;

3. To delineate and evaluate the reasons for, and the ramifications of, widespread exclusions of members of minority groups and the fears about the impact of their presence upon the mainstream of intellectual life, institutional practice, and other aspects of American culture;

4. To explore ways of enlarging the place of humanity, ethnicity, and individuality in the search for a deeper and clearer meaning to life in America;

5. To examine and criticize the causes and effects of the institutionalization of racial or color inequality in Western culture;

6. To investigate and analyze the philosophies and strategies for achieving the freedom and equality of non-White minority groups in a White majority culture;

7. To develop media and methods for educating members of minority groups more adequately, recognizing that the culture and conditions of minority group life often do not conform to those of the majority group life;

8. To recognize the creative aspects of a subculture in music, literature, drama, dance, and other forms of expression;

9. To study policies and plans for dealing with the problematic aspects of life in America in relation to non-Whites, especially with respect to discrimination, poverty, slums, ghettoes, and the like;

10. To bring together faculty and students with diverse talents and backgrounds, who, with sufficient financial and material resources, might cultivate a more probing and insightful education than conventional programs and institutions seem to permit.[41]

Three years later, in a special issue of the journal the *Phi Delta Kappan* specifically devoted to "The Imperatives of Ethnic Education," James A. Banks argued that ethnic studies was essential to an American society that was descending into near chaos from pollution, conflict over the Vietnam War, poverty, failing cities, and "ethnic conflict." Banks noted that immigrants of European origin successfully integrated into American society but those of "Black, Brown, Red, and Yellow" origin have been routinely denied opportunity in America. He further observed that schools, in this case apparently public primary and secondary schools, reinforced this White status quo. He argued that such schools must be enlisted to change it and make room to value non-White students' backgrounds and contributions. Doing so would require that teachers undergo "attitude intervention programs" including things like "seminars, visitations, community involvement, committee work, guest speakers, movies, multimedia materials, and workshops," as well as psychotherapy.[42]

The calls for minority curricular representation that were happening in the early 1970s included demands for White ethnic studies programs. This was possible in part because of the way the civil rights movement had so effectively taught Americans to think of citizenship in group, rather than individual, terms.[43] To explain these White ethnic studies programs, one can turn to an issue of the *Phi Delta Kappan* on "The Imperatives of Minority Education," which included an essay titled "White Ethnic Studies: Prospects and Pitfalls." The author, Mark M. Krug, suggested that such White ethnic studies would examine the lives of Italian Americans, Polish Americans, Irish Americans, and Jewish Americans. This call for White ethnic studies, sadly, seemed to stem from conflict between White and Black citizens in the lower socioeconomic strata of American society. As Krug stated in his article, "Tensions between Blacks and White ethnic groups have intensified the racial conflict in large cities, including Philadelphia, New York, Boston, and Chicago. In these cities, Blacks are determined to escape from the ghettos and are moving into White Polish, Irish, or Italian neighborhoods whose inhabitants are too poor or too much attached to their ethnic enclaves to move to the suburbs." Krug quoted a leader of the Polish American community in Baltimore saying to the *New York Times*, "We anguish at all the class prejudice that is forced upon us. Ethnic Americans do not feel that Black people are inferior, but regard them as territorial aggressors on their residential and employment turfs." Class was the major driver of White ethnic studies, as evidenced in the statement made by a professor of urban affairs at Rutgers, Stephen N. Adubuto. In nearby Newark, tensions between Blacks and Italians had reached dangerous levels, largely because of poverty and exclusion from the fruits of American culture. Adubuto explained these tensions and the drive toward White ethnic studies, as quoted by Krug: "A lot of people confuse us with White Americans, which we are not. We are the working class people who haven't made it in America, like the Blacks, and we are still in the inner city competing with them." Krug went on to suggest that these complaints by White ethnic minorities led to legislation for ethnic studies centers around the country as well as the development of educational materials for schools and training for teachers around ethnic studies. In fact, Krug noted, the calls for White ethnic studies were so successful that a cautionary tale was warranted: "These developments have made leaders of the ethnic groups happy. Some are so elated that they seem to have lost a sense of proportion when speaking about the concept and role of ethnicity in American society. Unless good sense and intelligent restraint are quickly restored, there is reason to believe that general sympathy for the plight of White ethnic minorities may soon be dissipated." The particular overreach consisted of criticizing the "melting pot" idea, suggesting it was false or dead, and criticizing school leaders and "phony liberals" on college campuses. Krug opposed criticizing leaders of ethnic minority communities because such communities' experiences needed to be integrated into textbooks and the general narrative of American history.[44]

Of course, another major change to the college curriculum in the late 1960s was women's demands for women's studies programs, perhaps the most recognizable academic curricular revolution of the 1960s and 1970s. The first fully developed program appeared at San Diego State University (SDSU), which started offering classes in the subject in the spring of 1970. According to SDSU's website, "By the fall of 1970, [SDSU] had formally established the first Women's Studies program in the United States which offered 11 courses. In the spring of 1974 . . . the faculty developed an 18 unit minor, which was approved by the University Senate in May 1975. That same year the university officially established the Women's Studies as a department in the College of Arts and Letters. In 1983, the department began offering an undergraduate major in Women's Studies and thirteen years later, the department created a master's degree."[45]

A 1970 issue of the *Chronicle of Higher Education* provides a sense of the curricula in these programs. Students could take classes titled

- "Women in Comparative Cultures,"
- "Socialization Process of Women,"
- "Self-Actualization of Women,"
- "Contemporary Issues in the Liberation of Women,"
- "Women in History,"
- "Women in Literature,"
- "Human Sexuality,"
- "Status of Women under Various Economic Systems,"
- "Women and Education," and
- "Field Experience."

The author of this article, P. W. Seamas, explicitly connected calls for women's studies with calls for Black and ethnic studies. He explained that some of the questions being asked by those developing women's studies programs were, "Should men be excluded from teaching or studying the subject," "Should women's studies be a separate department, an interdisciplinary program, or simply a scattering of courses?" and "Can women's studies be primarily academic or are they sure to become militant and tied to women's liberation?"[46]

Similarly, an early issue of the academic journal *Feminist Studies* reported on the efforts in 1972 of scholars Christine Grahl, Elizabeth Kennedy, Lillian S. Robinson, and Bonnie Zimmerman at SUNY Buffalo to set up women's studies there. They discussed their decision to join an already existing, recent curricular innovation known as "colleges," which were meant to be small, interdisciplinary, innovative curricular experiments. The authors stated that they chose to join this structure because it meant getting a women's studies program up and running much more quickly than having to go through more conventional routes. However, one tradeoff was that "the collegiate system offers little possibility of faculty recruitment nor any assurance of promotion or tenure." The "college" was essentially a department with more freedom from a central authority, like a dean or provost, but fewer of the resources—faculty lines, promotion, and tenure—that a more conventional departmental structure might offer. Over the course of three semesters in the early 1970s, the program offered "forty-five different courses a year (1971–1972), with an average of thirty courses offered per semester." The authors described themselves and their work as "the theoretical arm of the feminist movement," which required a deliberate definition and development of "what we need to know and how to go about learning it." The gravity of their work required rejecting a distinction Seamas seemed to make between academics and politics, what these women called "a polarity that defines 'liberal' approaches to women's studies as those [that embrace] conventional academic values and 'radical' approaches as those that emphasize consciousness-raising." Grahl, Kennedy, Robinson, and Zimmerman further explained,

> Part of our program is involved in outreach and orientation toward the movement and our courses do serve a consciousness-raising function. But consciousness-raising is not radical education. In fact, conducted in a political and educational vacuum, consciousness-raising is neither radical nor education. It is the beginning, not the end, of what we do and the kind of awareness we try to promote, even at that introductory level, is one focused on concrete strategies. On the other hand, because our work has its roots in a serious social movement, we must begin to establish a serious intellectual foundation. We are struggling to understand and control our own experience and we have neither the leisure nor the power—much less the time—to pursue the kinds of questions acceptable in a department that lacks our immediate point of reference and commitment to the real world.

Some of the courses that met the goals of theory development and activism in the real world were "Women in Contemporary Society"; "Lesbianism"; "Black and Female: A Workshop in Black Women's Liberation"; "Women and the Welfare System"; "Sexism, Racism and the Courts"; "Theories of Feminism"; "The Political Economy of Women's Liberation"; and "Sex, Race, Class, and the Oppression of Women."[47]

As these scholar-activists were agitating for their own spaces in the hallways of academia, they and others were also pioneering new scholarly approaches that asked new questions and used new methodological and hermeneutic approaches. Such work was a hybrid of activism and scholarship that sought to break down barriers of theory and praxis in pursuit of social change, led by this new radical strata of society, intellectuals in the Laschian sense, those whose job it is to engage in cultural criticism. The origins and nature of this hybrid activism/scholarship is explored next.

CHAPTER 2

IDENTITY, POLITICS, AND IDENTITY POLITICS

THE RADICAL, LEFTIST EDUCATIONAL activism just chronicled was paired in the 1970s and 1980s with an explosion of radical cultural analysis and criticism that, among other things, provided curricular materials for these new programs, which came to be known collectively as "minority studies." This body of work was often concerned with identity and a notion of the political focused on understanding the role of power in human relationships. Such a notion of the political, developed out of this academic activism and criticism, was also explicitly against the conventional traditions of electoral politics and political parties. These understandings of identity and politics soon developed into the new cultural phenomenon of identity politics.

Identity

The concern with identity that was central to this academic cultural criticism/activism was well established among liberal/Left activists in the 1960s. It was a main focus of the "new radicalism" of student campus activists—the student radicals were "search[ing] for a psychic community in which one's identity can be defined."[1] Additionally, it was central to new thinking about women's place in society; in Betty Friedan's groundbreaking book *The Feminine Mystique*, she devoted a whole chapter to "The Crisis in Women's Identity."[2] Identity was a preoccupation of much of the postwar American cultural landscape, dominated as it was by psychoanalysis and Freudian thought. However, before the 1960s, the idea of identity had been circulating in the

West; American sociology and social psychology had been working with the concept since the 1950s. Additionally, it was a concern of Jean-Paul Sartre and Simone de Beauvoir as they responded to the horror of the Holocaust.[3]

No thinker was more influential in establishing the postwar American concept of identity than the German American psychoanalyst Erik H. Erikson, who is possibly best known for coining the term "identity crisis." By 1960, he had become an American public intellectual and something of a celebrity with a tenured academic appointment at Harvard.[4] Across different works, and borrowing from social anthropology and comparative education, Erikson theorized the role of identity development in young people ranging in age from late adolescence to the mid-twenties. Erikson developed a concept of identity that refers to both an individual and a group, or rather to how one develops individually and as part of a social/cultural group like a religion. Erikson suggested that identity "points to an individual's link with the unique values, fostered by a unique history, of his people. Yet, it also relates to the cornerstone of this individual's unique development." Further, he noted that the word "identity" refers to several different processes in the developing psyche of a young person; it can refer to "a conscious *sense of individual identity*" or to "an unconscious striving for a *continuity of personal character*." In the sense that Erikson used it, "identity" might also refer to one process in a larger "ego synthesis," and finally to "an inner *solidarity* with a group's ideals and identity."[5]

Particularly, Erikson often focused on the adolescent and early adult years of men who later became "great" in some capacity. During this time in an individual's life, one is "most painfully aware of the need for decisions, most driven to choose new devotions, and to discard old ones, and most susceptible to the propaganda of ideological systems which promise a new world perspective at the price of total and cruel repudiation of an old one." Erikson believed the system that best satisfied this late adolescent longing and identity formation was accurately described as ideology. He defined ideology as "an unconscious tendency underlying religious and scientific as well as political thought: the tendency at a given time to make facts amenable to ideas, and ideas to facts, in order to create a world image convincing enough to support the collective and the individual sense of identity." Such ideology is, among those most committed, "a militant system with uniformed members and uniform goals." With less commitment, ideology in an Eriksonian formulation is a "'way of life' . . . a world-view which is consonant with existing theory, available knowledge, and common sense, and yet is significantly more: a utopian outlook, a cosmic mood, or a doctrinal logic, all shared as self-evident beyond any need for demonstration."[6] In Erikson's formulation, this search for ideology and a "way of life" is a movement toward a stable identity that will then shape the subsequent adult years of the young man. Erikson posited that during this period of identity formation, cultures provide time and space for a "psychosocial moratorium" characterized by "extremes of *subjective experience*, alternatives of *ideological choice*, and potentialities of *realistic commitment*."[7] Such a description generally matches the student radicals described in chapter 1, students ranging in age from eighteen to twenty-two and attending four-year colleges and universities. Moreover, it further suggests that the postwar American university was a particularly hospitable place for the development of an identity based on adherence to a particular ideology.

Betty Friedan, long before she wrote *The Feminine Mystique*, went as a young woman to study under Erikson at Berkeley but dropped out early in her program. No doubt, though, Erikson's ideas influenced her thinking. In an early chapter of *The Feminine Mystique*, she described the problem women were facing in terms of this process of identity formation during the young adult years that Erikson chronicled at length in his work. She described winning a fellowship to study at Berkeley with Erikson and her own lingering doubt about whether a psychologist was what she "really wanted to be." Friedan noted in chapter 3 of her book, "The Crisis in Women's Identity," that women in the late 1950s had entirely given up the idea of a career, of using their education, and thus of continuing this search for identity in a crucially formative period in their lives.[8] Friedan theorized that this abandoned search for identity was a key sign of women's oppression or their status as subordinate to men.

The concern with identity traced here—formulated in Erikson's highly influential *Young Man Luther* and disseminated further and wider by Friedan's blockbuster tome *The Feminine Mystique*—would prove foundational in the coming years as a paradigm for those who were addressing major social injustices for women, homosexuals, Blacks, and other racial minorities, essentially the disparate groups that would soon be leveling strong criticisms of Whiteness, maleness, the West, and heterosexuality in their fight to receive recognition in American society.

Politics

The textual corpus of Leftist cultural critique that developed in the 1970s and 1980s alongside the radical campus activism of the late 1960s was explicitly, if not conventionally, political. A good example of this is Kate Millett's hugely influential 1970 book, *Sexual Politics*. This book explores how representations of the act of sex (coitus) in recent Western literature show differential relations of power between men and women, with women subjugated. In this text, the author provided a clear definition of what she meant by politics: "This essay does not define the political as that relatively narrow and exclusive world of meetings, chairmen, and parties. The term 'politics' shall refer to power-structured relationships, arrangements whereby one group of persons is controlled by another." She went on to say, "By way of parenthesis one might add that although an ideal politics might simply be conceived of as the arrangement of human life on an agreeable scale and rational principles from whence the entire notion of power *over* others should be banished, one must confess that this is not what constitutes the political as we know it, and it is to this that we must address ourselves." Millett sought to elaborate a theory of patriarchy and politics that defines power relations in terms of "well-defined and coherent groups: races, castes, classes and sexes"— put differently, according to physical and sociological identity.[9] The dismantling of patriarchy—particularly the White, Western one that she was writing under—was the goal of Millett's sexual politics. Millett's theory of sexual politics, then, was the idea that sex (either the act or the thing distinct from gender) as depicted in a few key works of Western literature reflects power relations between people of unequal power and illuminates the prejudices of White, Western patriarchy.

Millett's notion of politics here came from *The Psychology of Power*, published in 1966. Written by Ronald V. Sampson, this work insists that politics should be moral but that it is not; it is based solely on power, which cannot be moral. Power is "the production of desired consequences in the behavior or belief of another, where the intent to exercise personal ascendency is present in the one producing the effects." Morality, to Sampson, is defined as a "universal moral rule [that is] accessible to the human mind . . . [which is] the principle of human equality." He was generally critical of the state because he believed it was only concerned with power and not morality. From such a belief, he rejected the more traditional idea of the political as embodied in, say, electoral politics: "My general conclusion is that the belief in the possibility of advancing human welfare through working to secure political power is itself the most important single illusion which stands in the way of advancing that welfare."[10]

The text strongly asserts that there is one universal moral plane within which rests one moral law. This moral law is the idea that people have two choices—they develop themselves on the basis of love or on the basis of power. These two things, love and power, are oppositional, and one must necessarily choose one or the other—there is no interplay between the two. Further, motivation from either will weaken the interest in acting from the other; if you act from love you are not interested in power, and if you act from power you are not interested in love. Sampson believed that acting from love would foster equality in a culture and that acting from a desire for power would result in a society characterized by domination and oppression. Perhaps most importantly for the body of ideas that would develop out of this notion of politics, this struggle is absolute, all-encompassing. Sampson noted that

> the struggle between these dialectical forces is always the same. No one may contract out of it, however much he may wish to do so. For of necessity, everyone at all times and in all positions stands on a relation with other men which will be predominantly of one category or the other. In this sense, what happens in the world, what happens in history, inevitably reflects the contribution, active or passive, of everybody who participates in the in the vast web of human inter-relations. There are not diverse planes of reality to be judged by different standards.[11]

The "plane" he mentioned here was anchored on one end by Jesus Christ and on the other end by Adolf Hitler, with everyone in the world falling somewhere between the two.

Sampson's concern with the relation between power and morality appeared in an essay from the 1930s by Max Horkheimer, bureaucratic and intellectual leader of the Frankfurt School that so influenced student radicals in the 1960s. In an essay titled "Materialismus Und Moral" when first published, rendered as "Materialism and Morality" in a 1986 translation, Horkheimer criticized idealist philosophy for failing to consider morality. He sought to establish a materialist idea of morality that is "the life expression of determinate individuals." Materialist philosophy understands morality "in terms of the conditions for its emergence and passing away, not for the sake of truth in itself, but in connection with determinate historical forces." Most simply, Horkheimer suggested that "materialism understands itself as the effort to abolish existing misery." In the twentieth century, or in a place and time where and when critical thought is concerned with dialectical materialism, morality will be expressed in two ways: compassion and politics. The compassion individuals should express toward one another arises from the fact that, in the industrially bellicose West, "everyone is given up to blind chance. The course of one's existence has no relation to one's inner possibilities; one's role in the present society has for the most part no relation to that which could be achieved in a rational society." Human beings under such conditions are not "subjects of their fate"; rather, they are "objects of a blind occurrence of nature, to which the response of a moral sentiment is compassion." The political, in Horkheimer's formulation here, arises from a recognition that the order at a certain time in society is not fixed but is able to be transformed. In his time, a moral politics would transform current conditions to make them actually rational in the sense of Enlightenment rationality: freedom, equality, and justice. Idealist philosophy is a barrier to the realization of this Enlightenment ideal because it prevents value judgments, a claim Sampson echoed. Idealist philosophy sacrifices value judgments in its "unconditional respect for truth," understood as facts that can be proven via empirical evidence and positivism. Horkheimer argued that the intellectual world of the West in the 1930s was shaped by "human and cultural sciences" that did not "develop a connection with larger social objectives" but rather "establish and classify 'theory-free' facts." Horkheimer hoped to develop a morally oriented materialism that could be political, that is, could transform the current social conditions under industrial capitalism. Human and cultural sciences as presently constituted—focused on the "mere compiling of facts"—would be unable to inform this politics or efforts toward the transformation of the condition of society. Materialism suggests that, rather, theory understood as "a cohesive body of insights . . . stemming from a determinate praxis and out of determinate objectives" will be necessary to bring about the desired transformation.[12] In many ways, Sampson's text can be understood as a book-length exposition of this materialist morality that Horkheimer theorized in this essay.

The notion of politics established by Horkheimer and elaborated by Millett and Sampson—the idea that the political is about working, via cultural production or criticism, to illuminate and ameliorate inequalities between unequal constituencies—took off like wildfire among many academics, mostly humanists and social scientists, and especially literary scholars, in the 1970s and 1980s under the guise of "theory." Theory is an interpretive paradigm for cultural criticism that scholars began using extensively in the post-Vietnam era. Often, the politics of such academics involved using this new interpretive paradigm to do the political work of illuminating inequalities. Of course, the notion of politics outlined by Horkheimer, Millett, and Sampson resonates with the work of Michel Foucault, whose influence on certain corners of American humanistic and social science research in the post-Vietnam era cannot be overstated. Imported into America via, among other avenues, Edward Said's work and an overzealous history professor in California, power is the basic theme of all Foucault's work, especially the way state power impacts the human body.[13] A characteristic example of Foucault's notion of power comes from an interview he did after the publication of a highly influential work, *Discipline and Punish*. Of this work, Foucault said,

> This moment in time [of transition from penalty to surveillance in prisons] corresponds to the formation, gradual in some respects, and rapid in others, of a new mode of exercise of power in the eighteenth and early nineteenth centuries. We all know about the great upheavals, the institutional changes which constitute a change of political

regime, the way in which the delegation of power right to the top of the state system is modified. But in thinking of the mechanisms of power, I am thinking rather of its capillary forms of existence, the point where power reaches into the very grain of individuals, touches their bodies, and inserts itself into their actions and attitudes, their discourses, learning processes, and everyday lives. The eighteenth century invented, so to speak, a synaptic regime of power, a regime of its existence *within* the social body, rather than from *above* it.[14]

Foucault's ideas were used quite prominently by one of the earliest theory-oriented literary scholars, Edward Said, in his groundbreaking 1978 book *Orientalism*. Said chronicled a notion of Orientalism that "can be discussed and analyzed as the corporate institution for dealing with the Orient—dealing with it by making statements about it, authorizing views of it, describing it, by teaching it, settling it, ruling over it: in short, Orientalism as a Western style for dominating, restructuring, and having authority over the Orient."[15] Marxist thinking also had an outsized impact on theory-oriented literary scholars. Prominent examples of such works include Fredric Jameson's *Marxism and Form* and Terry Eagleton's *Myths of Power: A Marxist Study of the Brontës* and *Marxism and Literary Criticism*, two precursors to his runaway bestseller of 1984, *Literary Theory*.[16]

The use of Foucault and Marx in developing interpretive paradigms for much academic work in the humanities and social sciences, especially literary study, is one part of theory that took over English and other departments in the post-Vietnam era. But theory rapidly developed into a nebulous, chaotic, contested body of critical insight for literature and other cultural artifacts that had vague political definitions and great political aspirations. It is challenging, in the first place, to even define what theory is. Paul Berman described "theory" in 1992 as "supremely sophisticated expression[s]" of the idea that "liberal humanism is a deception. Western-Style democracy, rationalism, objectivity and the autonomy of the individual are slogans designed to convince the downtrodden that subordination is justice. . . . Despite the claims of humanist thought, the individual is not free to make his own decisions, nor is the world what it appears to be. Instead we and the world are permeated by giant, hidden, impersonal structures." There is one structure that permeates them all—language as understood through the theories of Ferdinand de Saussure. The authors who wrote subsequent theory—Jacques Derrida, Michel Foucault, Pierre Bourdieu, and Jacques Lacan—were, according to Berman, an "extravaganza of cynicism." Additionally, Berman wrote, "they were angry theories (though coolly expressed), hard to read, tangled, more poetic than logical." However, they were also "wonderfully expressive" and "modern art's extension into philosophy."[17]

As John Guillory explained it in his 1995 book, *Cultural Capital*, "theory" is a set of texts by writers like Jacques Derrida, Michel Foucault, Jacques Lacan, Jean-Francois Lyotard, Julia Kristeva, Friedrich Nietzsche, Sigmund Freud, Ferdinand de Saussure, and Martin Heidegger that "breached the disciplinary fortifications between literary texts and texts derived from other discourses, such as the linguistic, the psychoanalytic, the philosophical." By the 1980s, such writing had become a "canon of theory" to replace the more traditional canon of literary texts.[18] Another scholar, Valerie Cunningham, succinctly describes the confused importation of theory into American classrooms and its circuitous nature by claiming that theory is what you find in undergraduate theory courses:

> Structuralism and Feminism and Marxism and Reader-Response and Psychoanalysis and Deconstruction and Post-Structuralism and Postmodernism and New Historicism and Postcolonialism. . . . The modern gurus of Theory on these lines are, of course, the likes of Mikhail Bakhtin, Walter Benjamin, Roland Barthes, Louis Althusser, Jacques Derrida, Paul de Man, Jacques Lacan, Julia Kristeva, Luce Irigaray, Michel Foucault, non-anglophone thinkers all, but most notably French-speakers, the French men and women who poured the Word from Paris . . . into eager Anglophone ears from the 1960's onward.[19]

Still other thinkers see theory as a particular way of carving out an identity, an academic branding, as it were, a perspective that is evident in Francois Cussert's 2008 description of theory as a "weird textual American object . . . born between the two world wars or in the crazy 1970s, depending on historical accounts, but definable today as a strange breed of academic market rules, French (and more generally Continental) detachable concepts, campus-based identity politics, and trendy pop culture."[20] More recently, Marc Redfield in his book *Theory at Yale* describes theory as, "on the one hand . . . real and substantial institutional and discursive developments in literary and cultural scholarship in the final decades of the twentieth century, and on the other hand . . . mythologizing narratives and figurative constellations that partake of and cannot simply be teased apart from that institutional and discursive history."[21] Whatever else they may have done, these theories radically altered the intellectual life of the humanities in America by bringing an academic idea of the political into the study of literature and related cultural artifacts/processes.

This idea of the political advanced by theoretically inspired cultural criticism resonates with the idea of the political established by Millett and Sampson. For example, in the coda to his blockbuster bestseller *Literary Theory*, Terry Eagleton mused on "Political Criticism." Here he wrote, "I mean by the political no more than the way we organize our social life together, and the power-relations which this involves; and what I have tried to show throughout this book is that the history of modern literary theory is part of the political and ideological history of our epoch." This epoch was capitalist, and so political literary theory would function to point out the power inequalities created by capitalist economies. Resonating with Paul Berman's description of theory explored previously, Eagleton faulted liberal humanism, the dominant paradigm in literary studies to which political literary theory is opposed, for being complicit in the exploitations of capitalism. Eagleton claimed that liberal humanism was impotent, and that this was an example of a "contradictory relationship to modern capitalism." He suggested that the humanities existed simply to perpetuate the values of capitalism, and that "capitalism's reverential hat tipping to the arts is obvious hypocrisy except when it can hang them on its wall as a sound investment."[22]

One important political operation of theory is the one that simply points out that all positions are "political," that there is no un-political realm. More specifically, Eagleton observed, "I am not going to argue, then, for a 'political criticism' which would read literary texts in the light of certain values which are related to political beliefs and actions; all criticism does this. The idea that there are 'non-political' forms of criticism is simply a myth which furthers certain political uses of literature all the more effectively." Ultimately, it seems, Eagleton and like-minded critics engaged in theoretical criticism because they believed it would transform society: "Liberal humanist critics are not merely out for a more complete account of literature: they wish to discuss literature in ways which will deepen, enrich, and extend our lives. Socialist and feminist critics are quite at one with them on this: it is just that they wish to point out that such deepening and enriching entails the transformation of a society divided by class and gender." He further recognized that he was defending the work of "radical critics" whose examination of any cultural object—not just literature—would bring about the desired end goal: "human emancipation, the production of 'better people' through the socialist transformation of society."[23]

Another text that provides a good sense of the political ambitions of theory deployed in cultural criticism is Frank Lentricchia's 1985 text *Criticism and Social Change*. Here, Lentricchia suggested that he sought to write a book about "culture, intellectuals, [and] the authority and power of intellectuals—how intellectuals in their work in and on culture, involve themselves inescapably in the political work of social change and social conservation." The intellectual here is "the *specific intellectual* described by Foucault—one whose radical work of transformation, whose fight against repression is carried on at the specific institutional site where he finds himself and on the terms of his own expertise, on the terms inherent to his own functioning as an intellectual." Lentricchia's interest was specifically in effecting social change; he believed that "our society is mainly unreasonable [and] education should be one of the places where we can get involved in the process of transforming it." Lentricchia was focused particularly on the political impact of literary intellectuals, by which he meant "the sort of intellectual who works mainly on texts and produces texts: hence not only poets, novelists, and other 'creative' writers and literary critics in the narrow sense, but all intellectuals traditionally designated as humanists." Further, he focused on this "university humanist" because he thought "that his and her position as a social and political actor has been cynically underrated and ignored by the Right, Left, and center."[24]

Lentricchia imagined a literary intellectual whose radicalism was made possible by a "former traditional self," that is an immigrant or some other marginalized figure, having a "background outside the social, racial, ethnic, economic, gender-biased, and homophobic mainstream." The radical literary intellectual would "retrieve his outsider's experience, and bring it to bear in critical dialogue" with their mainstream position as a university professor. Expository writing and American fiction taught and criticism written from such a position was, according to Lentricchia, "our potentially most powerful political work as university humanists." It is the criticism that really seems the political act because

> "Criticism . . . is the production of knowledge to the ends of power and, maybe, of social change. This kind of theory of interpretation presupposes a critical theory of society and history" and such criticism will [produce] an image of history as social struggle, of, say, class struggle, an image that is not "there" in a simple sense but is the discovery of the active intellectual soul. This sort of interpretation, when worked through the traditional texts of the humanities, will, above all else attempt to displace traditional interpretations, which cover up the political work of culture. An active, self-conscious work of interpretation will show the political work that the canonized "great books" have done and continue to do.[25]

By the mid-1980s, then, there was a quite consistent notion of "politics" or "the political" emerging from new critical work being done in some corners of academia, an academic politics, if you will. This notion of the political as academia has defined it, or this academic politics, holds essentially that the political is about working in some sense to illuminate inequalities between people, and that such illumination will have a salutary effect on the material world. Further, both the inequalities themselves and the forthcoming remedies are strongly related to language practices within a "discourse."

Identity Politics

Leftist thinkers and critics that undertook their critical activities in and around the university starting in the early 1970s combined the cultural fascination with identity, as formulated by Erik Erikson, to this academic notion of the political to develop a new phenomenon known as identity politics. The idea of an identity politics was made possible because the earlier terms of political activism were no longer relevant. Until the 1950s, activists framed their goals in terms of either "liberal-democratic principles of equal individual Rights and political participation" or a Marxist notion of "class conflict, economic exploitation, and workers needs"; gender and race activists in the early part of the century tended to appeal to the liberal democratic principles and labor activists tended to appeal to the Marxist ones.[26] From the 1950s forward, political activists started to focus on the political and psychological impact of a marginalized existence. This brought matters back to the idea of identity that had been growing in the cultural consciousness from the work of Erikson and others in the postwar period.

The earliest mention of the phrase "identity politics" I could find appears in "A Black Feminist Statement," an April 1977 document authored by the Combahee River Collective. The group sought to focus on the oppression of Black women, a choice "embodied in the concept of identity politics." Further, of the activism demonstrated by practicing identity politics, they noted, "we believe that the most profound and potentially the most radical politics come directly out of our own identity, as opposed to working to end somebody else's oppression. In the case of Black women this is a particularly repugnant, dangerous, threatening and therefore revolutionary concept because it is obvious from looking at all the political movements that have preceded us that anyone is more worthy of liberation than ourselves. We reject pedestals, queenhood, and walking ten paces behind. To be recognized as human, levelly human, is enough."[27]

Those who are building the critical/political tradition of identity politics all seek some kind of justice that has yet been denied to too many people in American society. It is often described as "social justice," a term that is central to a massively influential work on the question of contract theory within political philosophy: John Rawls's *A Theory of Justice*, initially published in 1971. Early in the book, Rawls argued, "Our topic is that of social justice. For us, the primary subject of justice is the basic structure of society, or more exactly, the way in which the major social institutions distribute fundamental rights and duties and determine the division of advantages from social cooperation." His goal was to set out and clearly define "a set of principles . . . for choosing among the various social arrangements which determine [a] division of advantages and for underwriting an agreement on the proper distributive shares. These principles are the principles of social justice: they provide a way of assigning rights and duties in

the basic institutions of society and they define the appropriate distribution of the benefits and burdens of social cooperation."[28]

Rawls set out to define justice and establish the rules for how
justice could be decided. He defined justice as "fairness," which, he
noted, "does not mean that the concepts of justice and fairness are
the same." Rather, "justice as fairness" means that "the principles of
justice are agreed to in an initial situation that is fair." In this scenario,
Rawls proposed that such an initial situation is one in which no one
knows where they belong in hierarchies of society and/or class nor
what kind of personal advantages they may possess such as intelligence or strength. This lack of knowledge creates a "veil of ignorance"
that is the only condition for a just social organization.[29]

As mentioned earlier in the chapter, the influence of Foucault on
literary and minority studies scholars is hard to overstate. The theory and practice of identity politics draws on his work in *The History
of Sexuality*, translated into English in 1978. In this book, Foucault
sought to provide a historical, "historico-theoretical," and "historico-
political" account of sexuality in the West. In so doing, he was working against an established "repressive hypothesis" of sexuality which
argued that sexuality up until the sixteenth century was open, free,
and plentiful, but beginning around that time, sexuality was closed
up behind doors of the male-dominated, heterosexual nuclear family and no longer spoken of. Foucault did not wish to *disprove* such a
thesis, per se; rather, he wanted to situate the thesis in a discourse and
examine the historical, political, and consequent power dimensions
of this discourse. As he put it,

> [My doubts about the repressive hypothesis] are aimed at . . . putting
> [the repressive hypothesis] back within a general economy of dis-
> courses on sex in modern societies since the seventeenth century. . . .
> The object, in short is to define the regime of power-knowledge-
> pleasure that sustains the discourse on human sexuality in our part of
> the world. The central issue, then, is . . . to account for the fact that
> it is spoken about, to discover who does the speaking, the positions
> and viewpoints from which they speak, the institutions which prompt
> people to speak about it and which store and distribute the things that
> are said. What is at issue, briefly, is the over-all "discursive fact," the
> way in which sex is "put into discourse."

Foucault wished to write the history *not* of sexuality, as the title of his book implies, but of *the discourse of* sexuality in Western societies, of the way sexuality is *constructed* as a linguistic phenomenon with theoretical, political, and cultural consequences. The physical act of sex itself exists of course, but Foucault argued that the physical acts took on a discursive existence in Western culture that fed into power relations between social actors. As an example of what this means, Foucault described how Catholic pastoral texts began to demand the description of sinful sexual acts and impulses at the same time that the culture demanded a new, more modest language when discussing sex. The language became modest and the discourse demanded by the church became explicit, unsparing. This tendency was taken up in "scandalous" literature—the Marquis de Sade here—and then made a part of the "public interest." This "public interest" was "power mechanisms that functioned in such a way that discourse on sex . . . became essential. Toward the beginning of the eighteenth century, there emerged a political, economic, and technical incitement to talk about sex. And not so much in the form of a general theory of sexuality as in the form of analysis, stocktaking, classification, and specification of quantitative or causal studies." One example of this power mechanism disguised as public interest was the idea of "'population,' as an economic and political problem: population as wealth, population as manpower or labor capacity, population balanced between its own growth and the resources it commanded. Governments perceived that they were not dealing simply with subjects, or even with a 'people' but with a 'population,' with its specific phenomena and its peculiar variables: birth and death rates, life expectancy, fertility, state of health." Foucault found sex "at the heart" of this "economic and political problem" of "the population" because of bureaucratic measurement of things like "birthrates, the age of marriage, the legitimate and illegitimate births, the precocity and frequency of sexual relations, the ways of making them fertile or sterile."[30]

French thought from the 1970s was influential in the formulation of identity politics beyond Foucault as well. This writing is often referred to as poststructuralist or postmodern, and it changed the terms in which identity was understood. Foucault, Jacques Lacan, and Jacques Derrida were united in their efforts to "deny the concept [identity] philosophical legitimacy." This was because before this poststructuralist work, identity had been understood in terms of master narratives like bourgeois liberalism or Marxism, which were tied to "Christian escatology."[31] For them, language, not identity, was the frame in which the human experience should be understood. This poststructuralist emphasis on language rather than identity, or how language constructs an identity, is evident in Hélène Cixous's essay "The Laugh of the Medusa," written in 1975 and translated into English in 1976. This piece urged women to write so as to develop a body of feminine writing. She implored women to "write, let no one hold you back, let nothing stop you: not man; not our imbecilic capitalist machinery, in which publishing houses are the crafty, obsequious relayers of imperatives handed down by an economy that works against us and off our backs; and not *yourself*. Smug-faced readers, managing editors, and big bosses don't like the true texts of women—female sexed texts. That kind scares them." She elaborated, "I say we must [write], for with few exceptions, there has not yet been any writing that inscribes femininity; exceptions are so rare, in fact, that after plowing through literature across languages, cultures, and ages, one can only be startled at this vain scouting mission. It is well known that the number of women writers . . . has always been ridiculously small." A woman's writing will be intensely physical: "Women must write through their bodies, they must invent the impregnable language that will wreck partitions, classes, and rhetorics, regulations and codes, they must submerge, cut through, get beyond the ultimate reserve-discourse."[32]

Another French feminist thinker important to identity politics is Luce Irigaray. Her book *This Sex Which Is Not One* is a collection of essays that bring the female into Western culture and philosophy. The book is deeply Freudian, discussing how psychoanalytic theory subordinates women's sexual function to men's sexual function, imaging women's sexual function only as a diminished or lacking version of men's. Irigaray theorized a "dominant phallic economy" in which women's desire was embedded in the hope or belief that she would, presumably metaphorically, acquire a penis.[33] This phallic economy was a central aspect of the Western construction of sexuality that emphasized a penile erection and a focus on visuals and form.

Irigarary believed that this Western construction of sexuality was foreign to female sexuality.

Many of the founding texts that informed our current practice of identity politics arise from second-wave feminism's academic arm struggling to achieve an accurate and inclusive understanding of women. As described at the end of the previous chapter, the nascent academic study of women and their place in society was, from the beginning, a pioneering mix of activism and more traditional academic work. Many of the early texts of identity politics reveal this activist-academic hybridity, concerned as they are with first directing the academic study of women and then, almost at the same time, challenging the White, heteronormativity of the earliest strains of second-wave feminism. Some of this is apparent in the writings of Cixous and Irigaray; another text that illustrates this is "The Homosexual Role" by British sociologist Mary McIntosh. Her essay was published in 1968, just a few years after the 1963 publication of Betty Freidan's *Feminine Mystique*. At the time McIntosh's essay was written, homosexuality was seen in the West as a "condition" that affected people, "in the way that birthplace or deformity might characterize them," identified by a medically sanctioned diagnosis of the condition. McIntosh argued that the concept of a homosexual medical "condition" was, in itself, a possible object of study: "This conception and the behavior it supports [attempts at empirical study via scientific methods] operate as a form of social control in a society in which homosexuality is condemned. Furthermore, the uncritical acceptance of the conception by social scientists can be traced to their concern with homosexuality as a social problem. They have tended to accept the popular definition of what the problem is and they have been implicated in the process of social control." McIntosh's ultimate aim, then, was to have "the homosexual . . . be seen as playing a social role rather than having a condition." She went on to write that "the role of the homosexual does not simply describe a sexual behavior pattern. . . . The purpose of introducing the term 'role' is to enable us to handle the fact that behavior in this sphere does not match popular belief: that sexual behavior patterns cannot be dichotomized in the way that the social roles of homosexual and heterosexual can." McIntosh tried to look to history to understand the homosexual role

cross-culturally and trans-historically but prefaced such an investigation by noting that the history might not be reliable because of the
bias of Western historians against homosexuality.[34]

Almost as soon as it was established, second-wave feminism splin-
tered. One critique concerned the heteronormativity of the nascent
movement, a conversation that was possible at least partially because
of McIntosh's work. Lesbian women had trouble with the existing
women's and gay rights movements because they felt both movements ignored their specific needs and concerns. To address such
oversight, the short lived Radicalesbians formed and produced a
collectively written essay, considered their "manifesto." Titled "The
Woman Identified Woman," it posits that a lesbian is "the rage of all
women condensed to the point of explosion. She is the woman who,
often beginning at an extremely early age, acts in accordance with
her inner compulsion to be a more complete and freer human being
than her society—perhaps then, but certainly later—cares to allow
her." The group echoed McIntosh's emphasis on homosexuality being
a role but took issue with the roles available to them: "lesbianism,
like male homosexuality, is a category of behavior possible only in a
sexist society characterized by rigid sex roles and dominated by male
supremacy."[35]

Another critique of the early second-wave women's movement
sought to draw on Marxian thought. Exemplary of this is Shulamith
Firestone's *The Dialectic of Sex*, published in 1970. This text was an
attempt to inspire a revolution in women's social position that was
analogous to the economic and social revolutions Marx and Engels
imagined in their critique of capitalism. Firestone was particularly
interested in Marx and Engel's "analytic method," which essentially
meant "a materialist view of history based on sex itself." In place of
class, Firestone substituted gender. Firestone's aim for this radical
feminist revolution was to "overthrow [the] oldest, most rigid class/
caste system in existence, the class system based on sex—a system
consolidated over thousands of years, lending the archetypical male
and female roles an underserved legitimacy and seeming perma-
nence." Firestone was, like Millett and Sampson, working from a
definition of politics that was critical of conventional political life,
focusing on "legal inequities, employment discrimination and the

like." Instead, her goal was for radical feminists to engage in a kind of politics that accomplished "liberation from sex roles altogether or radical questioning of family values."[36]

The feminist movement Firestone sought to cultivate would work from a "new political style" in which the personal and the political were intertwined. Firestone wrote, "The feminist movement is the first to combine effectively the 'personal' with the 'political.' It is developing a new way of relating, a new political style, one that will eventually reconcile the personal—always the feminine prerogative—with the public, with the 'world outside,' to restore that world to its emotions, and literally to its senses." Additionally, this "revolutionary feminism is the only radical programme that immediately cracks through to the emotional strata underlying 'serious' politics, thus reintegrating the personal with the public, the subjective with the objective, the emotional with the rational—the female principle with the male."[37] Firestone was describing here, without naming it, an activism based on identity politics—this idea that women will act on behalf of women to change the cultural perception/position of the female population.

The Combahee River Collective that first used the term "identity politics" and that authored the call for a Black, feminist activism in 1977 was part of a wider movement seeking to draw attention to the focus on White women in the women's movement. One well-known contributor to this cause was Audre Lorde. In one of her more well-known essays, "Use of the Erotic: Erotic as Power" (1978), she offered a metaphysical and psychoanalytic meditation on the power of the erotic in women's lives. The erotic is "a measure between the beginnings of our sense of self and the chaos of our strongest feelings." It is also "an assertion of the lifeforce of women; of that creative energy empowered, the knowledge and use of which we are now reclaiming in our language, our history, our dancing, our loving, our work, our lives." Getting in touch with the erotic makes one less inclined to feel powerless and thus have the energy to be more conventionally political in the sense that one can attempt to change the surrounding structures. Lorde noted,

> This erotic charge is not easily shared by women who continue to operate under an exclusively european-american [sic] male tradition.

I know it was not available to me when I was trying to adapt my consciousness to this mode of living and sensation. . . . Recognizing the power of the erotic within our lives can give us the energy to pursue genuine change within our world, rather than merely settling for a shift of characters in the same weary drama. For not only do we touch our most profoundly creative source, but we do that which is female and self-affirming in the face of a racist, patriarchal, and anti-erotic society.[38]

Here Lorde expressed the critique of Whiteness, and the West, that was so central to the cultural work of identity politics.

Another participant in this movement for a Black feminist platform was bell hooks. Her 1981 book *Ain't I a Woman: Black Women and Feminism* is generally about how Black women have been systematically ignored and abused by the American economic and cultural apparatus because "institutionalized sexism—that is, patriarchy—formed the base of the American social structure along with racial imperialism." Of Black women's neglect in the larger American story, hooks wrote,

No other group in America has so had their identity socialized out of existence as have Black women. We are rarely recognized as a group separate and distinct from Black men, or as a present part of the larger group "women" in this culture. When Black people are talked about, sexism militates against the acknowledgement of Black women; when women are talked about racism militates against a recognition of Black female interests. When Black people are talked about the focus tends to be on Black *men*; and when women are talked about the focus tends to be on *White* women.

Hooks also sought to critique existing feminist theory for being racist by ignoring Black women and being complicit in much of the larger culture's amelioration of Black women:

There exists in the language of the very movement that is supposedly concerned with eliminating sexist oppression, a sexist-racist attitude toward Black women. Sexist-racist attitudes are not merely present in the consciousness of men in American society; they surface in all our ways of thinking and being. All too frequently in the women's movement it was assumed one could be free of sexist thinking by simply adopting the appropriate feminist rhetoric; it was further assumed that identifying oneself as oppressed freed one from being an oppressor.

To a very grave extent such thinking prevented White feminists from understanding and overcoming their own sexist-racist attitudes toward Black women. They could pay lip service to the idea of sisterhood and solidarity between women but at the same time dismiss Black women.[39]

In 1980, the well-known poet/critic Adrienne Rich combined the analytic method of Kate Millett with the heteronormative critique of the Radicalesbians to write her widely influential essay "Compulsory Heterosexuality and the Lesbian Existence." This essay explores the representation of women's sexuality in literature. Rich looked to upend some assumptions about women's sexuality, namely, "first, how and why women's choice of women as passionate comrades, life partners, co-workers, lovers, tribe, has been crushed, invalidated, forced into hiding and disguise; and second, the virtual or total neglect of lesbian existence in a wide range of writings, including feminist scholarship." Rich made clear that the object of her critique was feminist theory and criticism:

> My organizing belief is that it is not enough for feminist thought that specifically lesbian texts exist. Any theory or cultural/political creation that treats lesbian existence as a marginal or less "natural" phenomenon, as mere "sexual preference," or as the mirror image of heterosexual or male homosexual relations is profoundly weakened thereby, whatever its other contributions. Feminist theory can no longer afford merely to voice a toleration of "lesbianism" as an "alternative lifestyle" or make a token allusion to lesbians. A feminist critique of compulsory heterosexual orientation for women is long overdue.[40]

When Rich wrote this essay, the second-wave women's movement was not even twenty years old, and it was clear that a significant part of it involved the critique of culture. Further, we can easily see the imprint of an academic politics concerned with revealing the discrimination one identity group—lesbian feminist critics—experienced at the hands of another identity group: heteronormative feminist critics that had achieved a (somewhat) mainstream presence.

Almost immediately after Rich's critique was published, an edited collection appeared that was also aimed at the cultural work of the feminist movement but which was concerned with a critique of Whiteness generally. Edited by Cherríe Moraga and Gloria

Anzaldúa, the collection was titled *This Bridge Called My Back: Writings by Radical Women of Color*. Organized into six parts and containing a combination of artwork, poetry, testimonials, and essays, this collection examines the tyranny and pressure of Whiteness as a physical, bodily, and cultural ideal and the heartbreaking violence experienced by Asian, Black, Hispanic, and Native women. The book suggests that the childhoods of women whose work is collected in the book taught them that "survival" was about being able to pass as White, which leads to a "color problem. . . . 'not White enuf, not dark enuf,' always up against a color chart that first got erected far outside our families and our neighborhoods, but which invaded them both with systematic determination." These women all came from different places, different kinds of neighborhoods, but they all were "victims of the invisible violation which happens indoors and inside ourselves: the self-abnegation, the silence, the constant threat of cultural obliteration." The text describes the "theory" the book adheres to, a "Theory in the Flesh," which holds that

> the physical realities of our lives—our skin color, the land or concrete we grew up on, our sexual longings—all fuse to create a politic born out of necessity. Here, we attempt to bridge the contradictions in our experience:
>
> - We are the colored in a White feminist movement
> - We are the feminists among the people of our culture
> - We are often the lesbians among the straight
> - We do this bridging by naming ourselves and by telling our stories in our own words.[41]

Moraga contributed an essay to this volume titled "La Guera." In it, she vividly described growing up in southern California as the child of a Chicana mother and an Anglo father who struggled financially. Moraga was on a college prep path at school and was expected by her mother, who neither wrote nor read English, to have a much easier life than she did because Moraga was both educated and fairer-skinned. The pressure or expectation of this Whiteness, and the way it severed her from connections with her Chicana heritage, however, was what Moraga wanted to explore. She noted with distaste that she was "anglocized" by her mother's "desire to protect her children from poverty," because Whiteness would be an asset in the moneyed mainstream of America. Moraga described her "experience, daily, [of] a huge disparity between what I was born into and what I was to grow up and become," which was a lesbian. She further explained, "When I finally lifted the lid to my lesbianism, a profound connection with my mother reawakened in me. It wasn't until I acknowledged and confronted my own lesbianism in the flesh, that my heartfelt identification with and empathy for my mother's oppression—due to being poor, uneducated, and Chicana—was realized. My lesbianism is the avenue through which I have learned the most about silence and oppression, and it continues to be the most tactile reminder to me that we are not free human beings." The rest of the essay is an attempt to get all oppressed people—which seems in her framework to be anyone who is either not White or not a White man—to work together to overcome their oppression. First, she needed to address the difficulties faced by those who have multiple, possibly competing identity categories, a phenomenon that would later, in the mid-1990s, come to be known as "intersectionality." She commented,

> The joys of looking like a White girl ain't so great since I realized I could be beaten on the street for being a dyke. If my sister's being beaten because she's Black, it's pretty much the same principle. We're both getting beaten any way you look at it. . . . In this country, lesbianism is a poverty—as is being brown, as is being a woman, as is being just plain poor. The danger lies in ranking the oppressions. *The danger lies in failing to acknowledge the specificity of the oppression.* The danger lies in attempting to deal with oppression purely from a theoretical base.

Moraga was concerned here with one of the inherent limits of an academic politics based on identity: if one has multiple oppressed identities, which do you choose to fight on behalf of? How does one build solidarity? She continued,

> Without an emotional, heartfelt grappling with the source of our own oppression, without naming the enemy within ourselves and outside of us, no authentic, non-hierarchical connection among oppressed groups can take place. When the going gets rough, will we abandon our so called comrades in a flurry of racist/heterosexist/what-have-you-panic? To whose camp, then, should the lesbian of color retreat? Her very presence violates the ranking and abstraction of oppression.

Do we merely live hand to mouth? Do were merely struggle with "ism" that's sitting on top of our own head? The answer is: yes, I think first we do; and we must do so thoroughly and deeply. But to fail to move out of there will only isolate us in our own oppression—will only insulate, rather than radicalize us.

By way of illustration, Moraga offered the anecdote of a conversation she had with a gay male friend. The friend confessed that he was afraid Moraga didn't trust him and would kill him if their (presumably then mutual) political activity came down to activism-based gender war—a war between men and women. Moraga said she very well might kill him in such circumstances. Her male friend

> wanted to understand the source of my distrust. I responded "you're not a woman. Be a woman for a day. Imagine being a woman." He confessed that the thought terrified him because, to him, being a woman meant being raped by men. He *had felt* raped by men; he wanted to forget what that meant. What grew from that discussion was the realization that in order for him to create an authentic alliance with me, he must deal with the primary source of his own sense of oppression. He must, first, emotionally come to terms with what it feels like to be a victim. If he—or anyone—were to truly do this, it would be impossible to discount the oppression of others, except by again forgetting how we have been hurt.

Thus, the solidarity that Moraga was looking for, the banding together of oppressed people across possibly multiple categories of oppression based on identity, required a rather brutal self-reflection. It required that those in the "movement"—the women's movement, maybe, though also a general movement of oppressed non-White homosexual people against oppressing White heterosexual people— "seriously address ourselves to some very frightening questions: How have I internalized my own oppression? How have I oppressed?"[42]

The critique of Whiteness that is so central to identity politics is possible at least because of the critical work of Frantz Fanon. His book *Black Skin, White Masks*, originally published in French in 1952, was available in translation by 1968. Fanon was a Lacanian-trained psychiatrist writing about the experience of the colonized in the French Antilles. In this text he sought to illuminate the psychological colonization that takes place in the hearts and minds of those who are physically colonized. Thus, the goal of this text was not to make the case that Blacks and Whites are equal; rather it was to "liberate the Black man from the arsenal of complexes that germinated in a colonial situation." These complexes came, first of all, from the colonizers' culture that the colonized must adopt through the use of the colonizers' language. Fanon wrote that "all colonized people—in other words, people in whom an inferiority complex has taken root, whose local cultural originality has been committed to the grave—position themselves in relation to the civilizing language: i.e. the metropolitan culture." Fanon was primarily concerned with critiquing the racism inherent in European colonization and showing how such racism revealed European claims to "civilization" to be hypocritical. He made clear the connection between material well-being and "civilized" pursuits: "It is utopian to expect the Black man and the Arab [two colonized peoples] to make the effort of including abstract values in their weltanschauung when they have barely enough food to survive. To ask an African from Upper Niger to wear shoes, to say he will never become another Schubert, is no less absurd than wondering why a worker at Berliet doesn't spend his evenings studying lyricism in Hindu literature or stating that he will never be an Einstein."[43] Fanon's work was widely read and discussed in the post-Vietnam era by people looking to ensure equal treatment between White and non-White people.

The critiques of Whiteness, maleness, and heteronormativity that were underway were further developed by the White philosophy professor Marilyn Frye, whose various essays and lectures from the 1970s and early 1980s were collected in a 1983 volume titled *The Politics of Reality*. The titular politics never received an exact description, but she seemed to generally rely on the notion of the political as first expressed in Millett's *Sexual Politics*. For example, the "politics of reality" are about the power relations in a world that is inhabited, controlled, and defined by a kingly presence. Such a metaphorical kingly presence is an epistemology of White, male, heterosexuality that was dominant in philosophy in the early 1980s. The essays in this book offer early clear definitions and discussions of oppression, sexism, separatism, racism, and heteronormativity. In an essay on oppression, Frye tried to make a convincing, philosophical argument about why "women" is a category of oppression. Oppression is the metaphorical "caging" of groups of people that "has to do with your membership in some category understood as 'natural' or 'physical.'. . . If an individual is oppressed, it is in virtue of being a member of a group or category of people that is systematically reduced, molded, immobilized. Thus, to recognize a person as oppressed, one has to see that individual as belonging to a group of a certain sort." Women are caged by a "barrier" that is kept in place by men, mainly White men. This barrier "consists of cultural and economic forces and pressures in a culture and economy controlled by men in which, at every economic level and in all racial and ethnic subcultures, economy, tradition—and even ideologies of liberation—work to keep at least local culture and economy in male control." Another essay attempts to work out a definition of sexism, which Frye described thus:

> The term "sexist" characterizes cultural and economic structures which create and enforce the elaborate and rigid patterns of sex-marking and sex-announcing which divide the species, along lines of sex, into dominators and subordinates. Individual acts and practices are sexist which reinforce and support those structures, either as a culture or as shapes taken on by the enculturated animals. Resistance to sexism is that which undermines those structures by social and political action and by projects of reconstruction and revision of ourselves.[44]

Frye wrote in this collection too about Whiteness and White supremacy. She sought to complicate the idea of Whiteness by decoupling it from skin color. She noted that "Whiteness is, it seems pretty obvious, a social or political construct of some sort, something elaborated upon conceptions of kinship or common ancestry and upon ancient ethnocentric associations of good and evil with light and dark." She went on to describe how being White or Whiteness is ultimately about having the power to define what is White and what is not. She closed this meditation by claiming that "in a certain way it is true that being White-skinned means that everything I do will be wrong—at the least an exercise of unwarranted privilege—and I will encounter the reasonable anger of women of color at every turn. But 'White' also designates a political category, a sort of political fraternity." Finally, she anticipated the recent work of Ibram X. Kendi when she laid out the binary of racist and antiracist activity: "There is a correct line on the matter of White racism which is, in fact, quite correct, to the effect that as a White person one must never claim not to be racist, but only to be anti-racist. The reasoning is that racism is so systematic and White privilege so impossible to escape, that one is, simply, trapped."[45]

By the late 1980s, the academic arm of the women's movement was well established, and traditional disciplines like political philosophy were beginning to see the impact of the identity politics paradigm. A classic example is Carole Pateman's *The Sexual Contract*, published in 1988. Pateman is a political philosopher, and her goal with this text was to make a feminist intervention in traditional contract theory. She was arguing for patriarchy as a specific historical development that came out of classical contract theory, which in Pateman's argument developed a sexual rather than a social contract. Patriarchy, as Pateman defined it, is a specific form of political power that arose in the early modern period; from this, classical contract theory developed as a way of making sense of Western social formations in the early years of capitalist development. Classical contract theory adhered to an origin story that "tells a modern story of masculine political birth. The story is an example of the appropriation by men of the awesome gift that nature has denied them and its transmutation into masculine political creativity."[46] Females, or the feminine, have been written out of classical contract theory because they were assumed by all classical contract theorists except Hobbes to be subordinate to men.

Finally, in 1989, another political theorist came out with a book that showed the influence of the academic political critical movement under examination here. Titled *Identity Politics: Lesbian Feminism and the Limits of Community* by scholar Shane Phelan, this book is self-consciously writing in a tradition the author called "lesbian feminism." She sought to establish a politics specifically for the lesbian community. Such work was necessary because, as Phelan explained,

> Lesbians are one group among many that perceive and protest an intimately experienced oppression. Clearly, their sense of oppression is not operative solely at the level of laws, but is derived everywhere from a culture that presumes heterosexuality as the biological, psychological, and moral standard. Lesbians are silenced by laws defining their

sexual behavior as criminal; they are forced into hiding on the job, in housing, in custody battles, and elsewhere; they are ignored by tax and probate laws. These issues and others are increasingly common topics for legislation and debate within the United States and are, in a way, reminiscent of the civil rights battles of Blacks and women.

Lesbians along with the New Left rejected liberalism because "liberalism fails to account for the social reality of the world: through a reliance upon law and legal structure to define membership, through individualism, through its basis in a particular conception of rationality."[47] Consequently, lesbian feminists had to develop a new political theory that described their collective concerns.

Phelan, in constructing a lesbian feminism, argued that "the fundamental issue for lesbian feminism has been that of lesbian identity. The construction of a positive identity requires a community that supports that identity." Accordingly, she suggested that lesbian feminism should be "understood, simultaneously as the reflection of a particular understanding of the position of all women, as the theoretical formulation of lesbian identity, and/or as the new logic of inclusion/ exclusion with its own foci for control." Phelan discussed the movement's focus on language as a political act when she described the need for radical feminists to reclaim their female energy. Phelan elaborated, "The reclamation of one's female energy, of 'gynergy' if you will, requires a thorough-going examination and rejection of the male, necrophillic element in one's internal and external worlds. The recognition by contemporary theorists, philosophers, and students of society of the fundamental role of language in the structure of our worlds is matched in lesbian feminism, and this recognition has made the construction of alternate discourses and languages central to the project of building a home." Phelan then pointed to the work of another lesbian feminist, Mary Daly, who "engage[s] deliberately and painfully in a process of redefining and renaming the world around her: 'Since the language and style of patriarchal scholarship cannot contain or convey the gynergy. . . . I invent, dis-cover, re-member words.' She shares this with many other lesbian feminist scholars and poets: this project is seen as crucial."[48]

We see here the strong influence of Foucault's thought on Daly and the lesbian feminist movement. The focus on power and control, especially as it is wielded through language, was a primary concern for Foucault. Consequently, early lesbian feminists who were building the movement zeroed in on the word "lesbian" in their linguistically tinged political project to accomplish "cultural reconstruction." This cultural reconstruction occurred through challenging and changing the meaning of the word "lesbian" to cease to refer to women who have sex with women and to redefine it to mean someone who is necessarily political and working on behalf of a lesbian political movement. Phelan quoted from the work of a scholar named Jacquelyn Zita, who argued that "the point of definition is not simply academic accuracy or the opening of a new terrain of study, but is political." Still another scholar, Ann Ferguson, who was working on a similar project of language redefinition on behalf of the lesbian feminist community, offered the following definition of "lesbian": "Lesbian is a woman who has sexual and erotic-emotional ties primarily with women or who sees herself as centrally involved with a community of self-defined lesbians whose sexual and emotional erotic ties are primarily with women; and who is herself a self-identified lesbian." Of the various attempts to redefine lesbianism in the lesbian feminist community, Phelan noted that all of the newer definitions demoted the sexual act in defining lesbianism and favored instead emotion. Phelan explained, "What is central to lesbianism now [after all the attempts at redefining lesbianism] is, not the act, but the emotion; or, rather, not the sexual act but the verbal, emotive, and political acts." In sum, Phelan argued, these attempts to redefine the word "lesbian" were "strategic moves on the part of these thinkers, attempts to define and locate a community, and simultaneously, inevitably, to proscribe standards for it. Definitions are political events, and as such they can be evaluated not simply by correspondence to some preexisting reality, but require an analysis of both motivation and of (perhaps unseen) implication."[49] Ultimately, Phelan summed up the efforts of the lesbian community to redefine "lesbian" by making connections with the political theory of the new Left and 1960s campus activists.

The phenomena just chronicled—campus activism, a new mode of scholarship—could be argued to have had a negligible effect on American society at large. After all, this was an age before the internet and social media when nothing close to a majority of Americans went to college. Indeed, this would be a valid criticism. Almost no one attends to the vast majority of academic scholarship, and many people, including sometimes enrolled students, are deeply confused about what goes on in the ivory tower. However, these academic developments did, I argue, have a profound effect on American culture for two main reasons. One, attainment of bachelor's degrees exploded from 1960 to 1990. There was a greater than 100 percent increase in the number of bachelor's degrees awarded between 1960 and 1970, followed by an approximately 15 percent increase in 1970–1980 and a 12 percent increase in 1980–1990.[50] Two, identity politics was simplified to an academic "holy trinity"—race, class, and gender—for teaching undergraduate populations. The late 1980s and early 1990s saw several curricular battles over the undergraduate curriculum generally, and a "race, class, gender" interpretive paradigm more specifically, being imposed on various parts of the undergraduate curriculum, the place where such doctrine would have the widest impact. These curricular battles came to be known as the "canon wars." The next two chapters explore the canon wars and two particularly heated curricular battles, one at Stanford University in 1988 and one at the University of Texas, Austin in 1990.

CHAPTER 3

THE CANON WARS AND IDENTITY POLITICS AT STANFORD

ON MARCH 31, 1988, the faculty senate of Stanford University met and voted on a curricular change to the university's core, or general education, requirement. At issue was "Area One" of the general education requirements—also known as the humanities general education requirement, a three-quarter, year-long class that examined Western civilization from a variety of perspectives. Some students and faculty at Stanford wanted to discard the focus on the West and replace it with a different course, at least part of which would focus less on Western, European, male ideas and more on the perspectives of the global world and minority communities—women and non-White communities.

Without doubt, faculty senate meetings were taking place, across the country on that and any other day—yet months before the meeting at Stanford, national publications like the *New York Times*, *Washington Post*, and *Wall Street Journal* anticipated the vote. For example, on January 19, 1988, Richard Bernstein, a special assignment reporter for the *New York Times*, reported,

> At Stanford University, they still talk of the day nearly a year ago when some 500 students, on a march with the Rev. Jesse Jackson, came up with a slogan for the next generation. The students were celebrating a new course at Stanford, one that would stress the contributions of minorities and women to Western culture, and, they chanted: "Hey hey, ho ho, Western culture's got to go." Students and faculty members these days assert that the slogan expressed no hostility to the likes of Plato and Saint Augustine, Rousseau and John Stuart Mill, all of

whom are on Stanford's current list of required reading for freshmen. But in claiming a kind of equal time for minority contributions to American civilization, the chant did reflect a demand that is expected to be accepted by the faculty in the weeks ahead. Responding to charges that the core reading list reflects what some have referred to as a "European-Western and male bias" and what others call "sexist and racist stereotypes," the Stanford faculty seems likely to approve a measure that would eliminate the Western culture course that is required of all freshmen.[1]

Two days later, on January 21, 1988, an editorial by a Stanford undergraduate student named Isaac Barchas appeared in the *Wall Street Journal*. Barchas, a classics major, was deeply troubled by the proposed curricular changes. He felt that the Western culture course that was about to be voted out was essential for the maintenance of our political ideals. He wrote, "The idea of liberty that defines and animates the world's democracies is a consequence of the Western, intellectual tradition. How much longer can we cling to 'liberty' (or 'justice' or 'democracy') when our brightest young people no longer recognize the peculiar conditions, intellectual and historical, that permit it to exist? This informed comprehension for higher ideals allows us to speak of 'freedom' as something more than, say, a mere Leninist slogan." Barchas went on to describe the motivation for the change as not "academic" but "political," and pointed particularly to the Marxism that had influenced the social sciences for the proposed curricular changes.[2]

Of course, March 31 came, Stanford faculty voted, and the change much feared by Bernstein and Barchas and others was made. As *Time* reported on April 11, the vote represented "a compromise revision of their canon. This fall the original 15 books, all of them written by White, Western males, will be pared down. Out goes Homer, as well as Darwin and Dante. The six new requirements are unspecified works from Plato, the Bible, St. Augustine, Machiavelli, Rousseau and Marx. Next year Stanford's Western Culture Program will be formally replaced by CIV." The new program would require that students "read works 'from at least one' non-European source chosen by the professor." Further, the new legislation took the somewhat unusual step of mandating a sort of interpretive paradigm in its charge that teachers give "substantial attention to issues of race, gender and class."³

Very quickly, there was backlash against this vote. On April 19, the *Washington Post* reported on the fury of William Bennett, the U.S. secretary of education, regarding the change. Bennett lambasted Stanford, claiming that the change "was not a product of enlightened debate, but rather an unfortunate capitulation to a campaign of pressure politics and intimidation. . . . For a moment a great university was brought low by the very forces which modern universities came into being to oppose—ignorance, irrationality and intimidation," a charge with which the now famous Peter Thiel, then a Stanford junior and editor of the *Stanford Review*, agreed.⁴ On April 22, Charles Krauthammer, a well-known conservative editorial writer for the *Washington Post*, wrote an editorial decrying the changes. In it, he supported the idea of studying non-Western cultures but was concerned about doing so at the expense of studying Western culture. He argued that "affirmative action for people is problematic but, on the whole, a good thing: it gives those who were denied opportunity an extra chance to compete. Affirmative action for great books is an embarrassment."⁵

The controversy caused by the proposed changes and affirmative vote were a central episode in loud national controversies that raged over the college literary and humanities curriculum in the late 1980 and early 1990s. Eventually called the "canon wars," this was a loud, public, somewhat hysterical, ideological conflict about which specific texts would be taught in college English and general education courses and the interpretive paradigms used for those texts. For example, a characteristic question might be whether humanities courses and general education programs ought to require students to read Rousseau's *Social Contract* to understand the greatness of the man and/or his ideas or Ntozake Shange's *for colored girls* to understand Black, female subjectivity as formed by centuries of oppression. The canon wars of the 1980s have heretofore been understood as one of the liberal/conservative cultural battlegrounds of the last century. In reality, they were a fight between a group of cultural elites who were mostly political moderates against the impending, then-radical social changes wrought by the academic curricular activism of the previous two decades. The so-called canon wars, of which the Stanford episode was perhaps the best-known example, indicated the extent to which higher education had become by the 1980s the "headquarters of the larger culture."[6]

The canon wars began with criticisms of general education programs, English departments, and the new theoretical paradigms in use there, in this case deconstruction. In the early 1980s, a certain type of article began appearing in major newspapers, popular magazines, and scholarly journals. These essays were bound not by argument, nor by political ideology, nor by publication venue, but by a sort of rhetorical outrage framing similar, loosely affiliated topics: the profession of English studies and English departments and the object of study therein, the general curricula of colleges and universities, and the place literature has there. For example, in 1980, the *National Review* published two such articles. One by Jeffrey Hart, a professor of English at Dartmouth, faults Dartmouth for failing to develop and adopt a sufficiently cohesive and historical general education program, such as the one at Columbia College in the earlier twentieth century that became the inspiration for the "Great Books" movement.[7] The other, by Russell Kirk, laments the closure of such humanities programs at a few colleges around the country and urges colleges and universities to adopt such programs in the future.[8] However, a concern with unified core knowledge that would provide values, shape the soul, and ennoble one's adult life was not the concern solely of the conservative press in 1980. *US News and World Report* published an interview with Steven Mueller, the president of Johns Hopkins University, who argued that universities produced "highly skilled barbarians." Mueller suggested that colleges and universities focused too much on professions and vocations and not enough on humanistic education that would provide a "social consensus," a code of values to live by, and the ability to clearly communicate in writing and speaking.[9] Similarly, in August and September 1981, a two-part, thirty-page tour de force appeared in *Harper's Magazine*. Titled "Panic among the Philistines," this essay rails against the "postwar cultural establishment" for its adolescent obsession with explicit sexual depictions in artistic production and its refusal of any artistic standards. The cultural establishment he referred to was made up of popular novelists, writers, and playwrights; the writers and editors of literary magazines; and English professors, particularly professors of creative writing. The author was especially unsettled by ignorance of artistic criteria coming from a Western, humanistic tradition that would judge a work of art based on its style, intelligence, and ethical statements.[10]

Similar complaints and criticisms continued to appear in the popular press as the 1980s unfolded. In 1982, the *Baltimore Sun* published what would soon become a cliché of the canon wars: an attack on the irrelevance and absurdity of the Modern Language Association (MLA) conference, the main (and enormous) professional conference of English and world language professors. The author, Peter Jay, wrote about the "current level of absurdity" in the institutional study of literature on display at the MLA, exemplified by papers discussing "lesbian feminist poetry in Texas" and "the Trickster figure in Chicano and Black literature." Jay argued for the same commitment to a generalized, humanistic view of literature that was expressed in essays in *Harper's*, *National Review*, and *US News and World Report* a few years earlier. He wrote that such topics are not "the study of literature, which is really the study of life itself as seen by writers of skill and vision."[11] Later in 1982, in the *Washington Post*, Jonathan Yardley published an article criticizing the excessive specialization and professionalization of English professors. At issue was the publication of a minor work by Virginia Woolf that a professor of English and women's studies had put together. It was a recreation of the first draft of *The Voyage Out* compiled from various archival materials that Woolf had left behind. Yardley worried that such work "constitute[s] a violation of the author's own intentions" and believed such a matter must be addressed "in an age in which the scholarly specialists are systematically raking through the odds and ends of literature." Yardley questioned the value of such an endeavor, suggesting that it "owes its existence in published form not to the creative powers of the author but to the re-creative method of the specialist. My quarrel is not with the specific merits of [any given text] but with the general notion that anything exhumed by literary scholarship is automatically important and publishable—that it somehow enlarges and enriches our understanding of a writer's life and career. More likely what it enlarges and enriches is our appreciation of a particular specialist's zeal and ingenuity."[12]

Jay's and Yardley's ire was raised by an essay that had recently been published in *Harvard Magazine* by a Harvard English professor, W. Jackson Bate. Titled "The Crisis in English Studies," this article suggests English studies were in a state of crisis because of the confluence of four factors that shaped English departments from the 1880s to the 1950s: the potential breadth of the subject of English, the renaissance ideal of the *litterae humanories*, Romanticism, and the specialization of the professoriat. Bate would rather see English embrace the Renaissance ideal of the *litterae humanories* as its "core," "tak[ing] the experience of the classical world and putting it into a larger historical perspective and intermeshing literature, history, and philosophy [to create] that mysterious, all important thing called character as well as the generally educated mind." Further, he believed that such an approach to English would vivify yet another classical ideal: "a trust in the moral and educative effect on human character of knowledge." Bate noted that in recent years, English studies had tried to save itself from certain oblivion by two contradictory developments. The first was that English departments engaged in a sort of hostile takeover of different disciplines in order to increase their influence. One characteristic of this trend was

> the scores of "new courses" [in which] the traditional allies, history and philosophy, were avoided as unnecessary demands that interfered with the popularity so eagerly desired. Subjects that seemed to fit into current enthusiasms were torn from context and treated in isolation. Women writers who had worked, with pride, in larger literary traditions were snatched arbitrarily—whether major or minor—and a field overnight was created in "women's studies." The militant exclusiveness in focus of ethnic literatures is too well known to need comment, as is the sadness that excellent literature, among all minorities, should be treated in the isolation that liberal minded people deplore.

The other effort of English departments to save themselves from oblivion involved seeking a "core" other than the *litterae humanories*. Such a core was made by structuralism and "that strange stepchild of structuralism known as 'deconstructionism.'" Bate was especially unsettled by deconstruction, which he claimed "unites structuralist concerns for very special kinds of pattern with what comes down to a nihilistic view of literature, of human communication, and of life itself."[13] Insofar as such things were understood as the exact opposite of humanism, Bate would certainly be unhappy with the developments he saw.

It did not take long for English professors to respond to these very public criticisms, though they responded to the critiques somewhat privately. English professors met articles in the *Washington Post, Baltimore Sun*, and *Harvard Magazine* with essays in scholarly journals like *Critical Inquiry* and the *Profession*, a publication of the MLA. In 1983, English professor Stanley Fish published in *Critical Inquiry* a response to Jay, Yardley, and Bate focused mostly on Bate and things Bate did not actually write. Early on in the essay, Fish made a point that would soon become a cliché of the Left in academia—arguing that Bate's ideas were "pernicious" and "political, even though, like most anti-professionalist polemics, it presents itself [as] a program for removing politics and political considerations from a realm that should be independent of them." Fish wrote that Bate "cites as examples of undesirable new courses and specialties, women's studies, gay studies, ethnic studies," which Bate did not exactly do.[14] Bate lamented the separation of these works into their own categories, out of a more universal humanistic story. Fish then went on to launch mostly *ad hominem* attacks against Bate that in no way engaged the arguments Bate was offering (a point Bate made in his reply to Fish, invited by the editors of *Critical Inquiry*).[15]

Helene Moglen, a professor of English at the University of California, Santa Cruz, writing in *Profession*, picked up on Bate's crisis rhetoric but she argued that the crisis stemmed from declining enrollments in humanistic study, fewer majors, fewer courses, and writing classes taking the place of literature classes. Moglen, however, attributed the crisis to a "new conservativism" exemplified by "intensely nationalistic" appeals to defense and needing to maintain a competitive edge. Moglen acknowledged the debate happening between English professors like Bate and Fish, suggesting it was a new version of the old debate between ancients and moderns, and acknowledged that English professors were living through a pivotal time when it was necessary to "decide whether we will line up with [William] Bennett and Bate as defenders of the great tradition—and the critical approaches of the past—or with those in our profession who see themselves as the vanguard: one battalion representing the development of new theoretical strategies, another standing for pedagogical innovation."[16]

Whatever responses English professors had in their specialty publications, a specific narrative about a core, stable humanities, focused on the West, inculcating values, holding back the narrowness of vocationalism, and opposed to a narrow, specialized, incomprehensible brand of literary criticism known as deconstruction, continued to be argued in the mainstream press. In March 1983, deconstruction received lengthy (and negative) attention in the style section of the *Washington Post.* The author posited a conflict between humanists and "alien" deconstructivists, and reiterated the criticisms of the English department leveled by Bate's "Crisis in English Studies." In agreement with Bate, the article cited Gerald Graff, who stated, "As if our society had not rendered literature unimportant enough already . . . literary intellectuals have collaborated in ensuring its ineffectuality." It also mentions M. H. Abrams's caution against embracing a deconstructionist view of literature "in which meanings are reduced to a ceaseless echolalia . . . intended by no one, referring to nothing, bombinating in a void."[17]

The academic study of literature continued to be savaged in the mainstream press. For example, the *Wall Street Journal* published an editorial in January 1985 titled "There Is life after the Humanities," written by a man with "nine years as a student and teacher in the English departments at two prestigious universities." He claimed that graduates of contemporary humanities programs were literate but not humane. Liberal arts departments were full of professors who were "nervous, jealous, and controlled by grandiose neurotics."[18] This writer was particularly incensed by the embrace of Marxism as an interpretive paradigm to the exclusion of doing good works for humanity like visiting nursing homes. Similarly, in February 1985, the *New York Times* published a favorable review of a new collection of essays by Joseph Epstein that lamented the state of American literature. This came partially from "the overestimation, by university English departments, of contemporary writing; the ubiquity, in those same departments, of arcane procedures such as literary theory and deconstructionism the increasing politicizing of art . . . the frequent compartmentalizing of books into categories such as Black, Women, Homosexual, with a corresponding overrating of their individual value."[19]

In and among these public lashings of English departments, there were a few notes about the new minority studies. An article appeared in the *New York Times* in June 1985 about Princeton, which had lagged behind other schools in the establishment of a women's studies program. The article notes that Princeton was remedying this mistake by developing a new women's studies program that was fostered by the hiring of two prominent literary scholars, Susan Gilbert and Elaine Showalter.[20] Not everyone would have lamented Princeton's failure. Many were concerned about the effect of bringing new perspectives into the curriculum via minority studies rather than by integrating marginalized figures into a general curriculum that everyone studied. Bate, in his "Crisis in English Studies," said as much and in 1984, an article appeared in the *National Review* by the Distinguished Professor of Judaic Studies at Brown University who wrote about similar concerns. In an article provocatively (and unfortunately) titled "Ethnic Studies, Campus Ghettos," Jacob Neusner explained approvingly that "universities make room these days for many more kinds of people than they did a generation ago: Catholics and Jews, Blacks and women, Puerto Ricans and Chicano, Asian Americans and American Indians, Poles and Italians—a long and varied list of groups whose background present to the study of the humanities in America a fresh and unprecedented experience of what it means to be human: religions not commonly studied before, literatures not ordinarily read, histories not regularly examined." Neusner named this development—the traditional humanities reshaped by new perspectives and participants—the new humanities. Neusner described how a consensus built between the traditional humanities and the new humanities in the 1960s and 1970s was falling apart. He described the consensus as

> insiders teaching private things to insiders, and everyone learning public things as they had always been taught. Everyone for a time accepted the compromise. The newcomers felt quite at home, as well they should, having never left their ghettos. The established humanities retained their ultimate governance. Making room for newcomers, they found themselves essentially unchanged. The old privileges

endured and did not even have to be shared. What emerged, then, through the 1970's was curricular tokenism, a kind of intellectual affirmative action. . . . Unhappily the easy compromise of the 1970's has fallen apart. The new humanities cannot sustain themselves within its terms, and the established humanities are no longer able to explain themselves. The newcomers are proving inadequate to the labor and the old-timers have fallen into bankruptcy.

Neusner then suggested what he thought could heal the current predicament: focusing on being good teachers and on gaining "legitimate entry into the intellectual life of the universities [by insisting] upon the same principles of reasoned discourse and public accounting for all propositions that always have framed scholarship and defined learning we deem worthwhile."[21]

So, the conflict over the core at Stanford, described in the opening paragraphs of this chapter, was ostensibly responding to curricular discontent that had been building throughout the 1980s. This conflict did not begin in 1986 as some contemporaneous accounts suggested. In fact, it began in the late 1970s when Stanford sought to revise its general education program and align some important parts of its program with the critical, humanistic values that so many people concerned with higher education were arguing for. In the late 1970s, there were many competing pressures for higher education generally and general education specifically. As explored in the first chapter, the 1960s fostered challenges to the "traditional" curriculum and a massive expansion of higher education, the beginning of what would become known as "mass education."[22] Further, a vocational imperative dominated educational conversations in the 1970s, the emphasis of which left many in nonvocational fields like the humanities and liberal arts nervous about their future viability. Added to this mix were projections, not unlike the ones we are living with today, about declining enrollments and what that meant especially for elite institutions like liberal arts colleges that were traditionally quite expensive.

Given all this, there were great concerns among all stakeholders about the shape of general education: whether it should take shape as a traditional, philosophically humanist education, perhaps delivered by those arguing for a return to a core curriculum that would impart a "common culture," or whether a recognition of diversity of perspectives and students made "core" courses and the "traditional" curriculum irrelevant or, worse, racist. Such questions had bedeviled American higher education since at least the early twentieth century. From the time of Charles Eliot's implementation of the elective system at Harvard in the mid-nineteenth century, there had been an ongoing anguish about the kind of general education students could receive with electives. There was a profound sense for much of the twentieth century that the elective system was unsatisfactory because it provided an education that was fragmented and contingent. Critics of the elective system wanted American college and university students to have an integrated, synthesized educational foundation with an explicit focus on some shared reference points and knowledge bases among students. The end of World War II made the stakes of such a goal much higher because of the large numbers of students who were returning to American colleges and universities on the G.I. Bill.[23]

The most ambitious and significant attempt to create such a core educational experience was exemplified by a landmark report on what American students should learn, *General Education in a Free Society*, published in 1945, also known as the *Redbook*. This report, written for the State Department by a committee of Harvard faculty, was widely considered the definitive statement on general education in the postwar era. It was a second attempt to deal with the shortcomings of the elective system pioneered in the late nineteenth and early twentieth centuries, the first being at Columbia University and the University of Chicago to develop a uniform core educational program in Western culture, which set the mold for the Great Books collections created in the 1950s by Mortimer Adler and sold by Encyclopedia Britannica. The *Redbook* sought to establish a general education consisting of a "broad background of knowledge and outlook that all citizens should have no matter their occupational intent. This usually meant an understanding of the basic problems and methods of inquiry in the social sciences, the natural and physical sciences, the languages, literature, and philosophy of the humanities and the arts."[24] *General Education in a Free Society* is a document undeniably informed by Cold War ideology that orients the end of liberal arts study away from the historical imperative to cultivate taste into a means by which to celebrate, and foster fealty to, a distinctly Western heritage. The texts that would establish that heritage are the ones that would be the focus of bitter debate only forty years later at Stanford. The document suggested that "great texts of literature" like Homer, Greek tragedies, Plato, the Bible, Virgil, Dante, Shakespeare, and Milton be taught in this category.[25]

The curriculum that came under fire at Stanford in the late 1980s was quite similar in both content and pedagogical design to the one outlined in the *General Education* document. Interestingly, the plan in the *General Education* document was never really implemented at Harvard; it was defeated from the start by the faculty. Addition- ally, when the general education curriculum at Harvard was reexam- ined in 1963, it was found wanting due to a too exclusive focus on the West and Western values. Many were vexed by such criticism, how- ever, because they thought that moving away from a Western focus in general education meant giving up on the hope for a common learning experience for students. Rather than trying to figure out a non-Western focus of common learning for all students, the Harvard faculty decided to abandon the goal of common learning altogether and admit classes to the curriculum based on a judgment that courses were "good, [and] 'innovative.'"[26]

In the late 1970s, general education was still a conundrum that no one seemed to have solved. In a speech predicting the shape of higher education in the 1980s John Sawhill, president of New York University and secretary of the Department of Energy, argued for a revised general education program that "conceptualized and inte- grated" knowledge. His ideal curriculum would deliver instruction in both traditional subjects like Victorian literature and "[the] pressing relevant social and scientific concerns of our time." He wanted such a curriculum to be less Eurocentric but was careful to distinguish that from "ethnicizing the curriculum," which he defined as having Ital- ian Americans study Italian culture or Puerto Ricans study Puerto Rican culture—what was called later in 1984 by Jacob Neusner, the Brown professor, "ghettoizing" minority studies.[27] Mark Ryan, a dean at Yale, wrote in 1980 about a crisis in the culture of elite, East Coast institutions arising from students too heavily emphasizing competi- tion and getting ahead for jobs and leadership positions. Students were not inclined to learn about themselves, and Ryan was disturbed by what he saw as a lack of impulse toward "self-realization" or "self-actualization."[28] Finally, two scholars noted that the nation had recently become very concerned with general and liberal education. They wrote about a 75 percent increase in scholarly and professional articles between 1970 and 1979 and found that one of the main thrusts of all general education reform was a tendency toward wanting to foster a shared culture. They also noted that another significant impetus for this increase in discussions of general education were concerns about the "overspecialization" of faculty.[29]

Thus, the charge of the Stanford Committee on Undergraduate Studies in 1976 to "propose a curricular requirement in 'Western Culture' that must be satisfied by every undergraduate students [*sic*] admitted to Stanford after the fall of 1978" was, at the outset, taking place in a contested context.[30] In 1976, a subcommittee of the faculty senate, the Committee on Undergraduate Studies (C-US), was asked by a dean to consider adding a Western culture requirement to Stanford's general education program. At that time, the committee declined to recommend this (1) because the general education program in total went some distance in offering education in Western culture already; (2) because of unsettled questions among faculty as to whether it was better to have firmer, more consistent requirements that students had to take or if it was better to let students have wide berth in what they would take and faculty wide berth in what they would teach; and (3) because of bureaucratic matters yet to be solved like staffing for such a program.[31] However, by the end of the 1977–1978 academic year, such matters had presumably been resolved because the faculty senate passed in May 1978 a resolution to implement a pilot program in Western culture and civilization as a part of the larger program in general education.

The pilot Western culture (WC) program laid out a course of study that was meant to offer a common educational experience to students and a common base of knowledge. The year-long, three-quarter sequences of study that would make up the WC program had to:

- "Include the study of a considerable number, and share a basic core, of primary works or basic texts" which the Committee on the Western Culture requirement would choose
- "deal with more than one national and linguistic sub-culture"

- "cover the entire spectrum of time from ancient to modern— perhaps with different emphasis on various periods"
- The sequences of study must also not be an introduction to major areas of study.[32]

The pilot must have proved successful because the senate voted to adopt the program in its entirety as an official requirement in 1979 to be implemented at the beginning of the 1980–1981 school year. However, even in 1979, it is clear there was some criticism from the "non-mainstream" modes of scholarly inquiry like women's studies, ethnic studies, Black studies, and so on. The term "non-mainstream" comes from Carolyn Lougee, the chair of the C-US, which had commissioned the study of the WC program and which had unanimously recommended adoption of it in 1979. Lougee would be a central figure in general education at Stanford for the decade to come.

Further, the recommendation to adopt the WC requirement in 1979 already bore the imprint of curricular dissatisfaction that had animated the campus unrest of the late 1960s and the identity politics that developed. For example, the report on the pilot stated, "The works on the core list [that made up the required reading list for the WC requirement] are almost all by White males. Important aspects of the development of Western culture are not represented by works on the list. Nor does the selection produce a natural emphasis on the roles of minority groups within Western culture, or the interactions of European culture with other cultures. These facts pose serious problems which have confronted the committee since its inception. What can be done to address them?" In response to the query about what should be done, the report responded with three points it wanted faculty to consider in approaching the problem of representation of minorities in the new WC requirement. The report cautioned, first, against putting too much responsibility on the WC requirement to solve the problem of minority representation. Second, the new program was meant to "expose students to important works of Western culture in their historical context, to help them to understand the ideas in those works and trace their influence. It is not an attempt at glorification or indoctrination. There is no contradiction in the idea of a Western culture program playing a positive role in an education that sharpens the student's appreciation of other cultures, or of the role of women, minorities, and assumptions about them in Western culture." Third, the committee wanted to stress that the goals of the WC program sought to provide all undergraduates with a common learning experience that would be useful later on "for courses that focus on the shortcomings of aspects of western culture, for courses that provide new perspectives on western culture, for courses that compare western culture with other cultures."[33]

The report addressed the issue of the dearth of women and other minorities in the required texts of the WC program. It stated that the Committee on the Western Culture Program had developed a subcommittee in 1977 "on the role of women and assumptions about women in Western culture," and that this subcommittee would lead the development of supplementary lectures on women's issues in partnership with an already existing Center for Research on Women and the dean of humanities and sciences. The report ended by reiterating the idea that the WC program should not bear the brunt of accommodating these new scholarly paradigms because the program represented "only a part of the Stanford requirements, and only a part of a Stanford education."[34]

Shortly after the resolution was adopted, Lougee discussed the process Stanford had undergone in various scholarly communities, descriptions that illuminate more exactly the criticisms of the WC program mentioned in the 1979 report. Lougee gave a talk at the 1980 American Historical Association conference that explained both her work in general education and the implementation of a WC requirement. In an essay composed on the basis of the talk, Lougee wished to explore "some potentially effective ways of ensuring that the movement toward core curricula and other forms of structured undergraduate experiences includes what are now called 'non-mainstream studies' in general and, women's studies in particular."[35]

Lougee had a decidedly balanced view of this new WC requirement at Stanford. She praised it because it "provides us with an important means toward some of our general education goals in that it is *the* course in which we nurture freshmen's ability to read critically, write coherently and discuss cogently. The greatest of its virtues is that it reinstitutes the study of the humanities as central to the undergraduate curriculum. Its greatest weakness, however, is that in this as in other Western Civ courses, women are few and far between." Lougee suggested that the reasons women did not appear in the WC curricula was because such curricula were built on Western humanistic traditions, which in various ways excluded them. The Western humanistic tradition privileged male activities because it was focused on training for civic life, where men were often the only actors; because it valued a type of selectivity based on excellence in a genre (drama, painting, philosophical argument, etc.). She argued that the humanities could imagine no other type of criteria expressing excellence in works created in a certain genre. Finally, the humanities were oriented toward universality, toward what binds together a learned class that explicitly tries to keep out cultural diversity. She explained, "Seeking the uniform substratum beneath diverse humankind, the humanities tend to devalue diversity and celebrate a unitary image to which all should aspire to conform: that of the cultivated, educated gentleman." She suggested that these were the beliefs that animated the humanities and the renewed calls for WC curricula in the post-1960s educational landscape. She said, "The ideals of responsible citizenship, firmly recognized canons of value, and the melting pot appeal to an academic world hit hard by the claims of diverse cultures with distinct criteria of values and particularistic loyalties."[36]

Lougee named some ways that women and their allies might deal with the masculine focus of WC requirements. At Stanford, she said the idea of creating a separate curriculum that dealt with women for those interested in that subject was rejected because it reinforced that women's studies need not be a part of the mainstream curriculum (the "ghettoization" problem). Then, an ad-hoc solution had been developed in which instructors focused on the "misogyny of the Great Works on the core reading list: the extent to which male authors asserted or implied female inferiority, how flawed their understanding of women's lot and real women themselves often was." She suggested that this was a perfectly good way to illuminate both the history of thinking about women and a particular way of looking at the history of these writers and the texts themselves. Ultimately, however, Lougee found this solution distasteful because, as she wrote, she was interested in women and not in "three thousand years of misogyny," and that this ad-hoc approach would not place women in the WC curriculum—it would just provide a study of women as they were thought about by men, which wasn't a sufficient corrective after all. She then explained a third, most desirable option wherein the WC curriculum was modified to include women. She elaborated, "Here the technique is to talk about women alongside men from a feminist perspective by finding the nodal points in the traditional narrative framework where comparative treatment of men's and women's experiences is possible, noting along the way the record's incompleteness regarding women, examining the power relations in the past which caused that incompleteness as well as what in the last decade or so has led us to recognize it." Ultimately, Lougee's goal was to develop a new epistemological framework for the humanities that was not so masculine. Such a framework would "free the humanities from the ideals of public life, disciplinary excellence, and human commonality" and orient the humanities toward a recognition of the role and value of private life; it would eliminate formal generic criteria as the marker of excellence in humanistic artifacts; and finally, it would eliminate the value of universality in the humanities and replace it with the values of diversity and plurality.[37] Lougee's suggestion about reforming the humanities was a third, powerful critique of humanistic study. At this same time, scholars embracing theory were condemning liberal humanism for its dishonesty and support of exploitative capitalist structures; just ten years prior, accomplished humanists were positing a new humanism that moved toward integrating new ways of seeing and experiencing the arts that novelist Daniel Stern had called postmodern in 1970.[38] Thus, in the early 1980s, a major conflict was brewing: while academic leaders were calling for a return to the traditional goals and values of a humanistic education, powerful academics (teachers and researchers) in the humanities were arguing for, essentially, shattering such traditional notions of the humanities.

Student dissatisfaction also developed after the 1980 implementation of the WC requirement. In 1983, a subcommittee of the Black Student Union (BSU), the African History Committee (AHC), wrote an editorial to the *Campus Report*, Stanford's internal faculty and staff newspaper, in which they objected to the Eurocentric perspective of the WC program. They noted that Carolyn Lougee and the president of the university, Donald Kennedy, had recently recognized the need to convene a meeting to discuss criticisms of the program. In this editorial, they offered a few preemptive suggestions for reform. One was a different book: they recommended for the program George James's *Stolen Legacy*, a controversial book first published in 1954 to very mixed reviews; the controversy over this book was revived in the 1990s as part of larger arguments over the Afrocentric view of history. The BSU-AHC also recommended a new track that could "retain its European flavor but also examine the influences on and evolution of human society. This track should explain that Pythagoras, Democritus, and Socrates got their ideas from African thinkers." The students called for Stanford to hire a new faculty member with areas of expertise in the African influences of European cultural objects. They concluded by saying that their ultimate goal was the elimination of "the unwarranted and unfounded glorification of one culture over another. Ultimately the Western Culture program should become a program in North American Cultures and study the contributions and interrelationships between the cultures of Native American, Euro-Americans, Chicanos, Asian-Americans, and African-Americans."[39]

Survey data showed that the vast majority of Stanford undergraduates were satisfied with the WC program. Nevertheless, criticism of the program grew throughout the 1980s. For example, some faculty were by the mid-1980s still unhappy about the representation of women and other minorities in the program. Apparently in response to this fact, Lougee reconvened the Western Culture Subcommittee on Gender and Minorities, a subcommittee of the Senate committee that oversaw the WC program. It is unclear how long this subcommittee had been moribund when it was reconvened in the winter of 1985. This subcommittee's general responsibilities involved "[clarifying] the nature of the Western Culture Program specifically with regard to the treatment of women, of minority groups, within the Western cultures, and of the reciprocal influences of Western and non-Western cultures." In a memo to the faculty teaching the WC program, the subcommittee stated that they had been working over the previous two quarters on a range of activities that spanned from creating new kinds of classes for the program to "a reconsideration of the Western Culture requirement per se." More specifically, the committee had developed the following ideas: assigning one book that all incoming students enrolled in the WC program would read in the preceding summer; compiling a list of specific books authored by women and minorities that would supplement reading already planned in WC classes; the development of background materials for existing WC courses that would "[pertain to] counter-themes and counter cultures within the Western tradition to assist faculty in presenting contextual as well as textual issues"; creating a faculty development class that might explore "theoretical, methodological, and pedagogic problems" that minorities face; and sponsoring lectures, debates, and student projects on minority issues.[40]

Following on this work, the 1985–1986 academic year saw quite a bit of activism regarding the WC program. In February, the *Stanford Daily* published an editorial by a professor of French, Raymond Giraud. In this editorial, Giraud made the argument that "civilization," rather than being a timeless universal experience, was instead a deeply ethnocentric one. He argued, "Programs in Western Civilization or Culture tend to be ethnocentric. They review the achievements of a society dominated by upper-class White males, which has developed a tradition of identifying its origins in the Judeo-Christian Bible and ancient Roman and Greek culture" that is likely inseparable from colonialism. Giraud then concluded that "a conspicuous problem of such programs stems from the contradiction of insisting that this geographically centered, sexually centered, racially centered, class-centered, and even religiously centered cultural package be imposed as *our tradition* in a society that claims to be color-blind, multi-racial, and sexually non-discriminatory."[41]

Giraud then pivoted and began engaging in the same *ad hominem* attacks characteristic of some members of the academic Left like Stanley Fish. Giraud took aim at anyone who would wish to plan programs in WC with language that evoked charging a criminal: "This brings us to the first change that can be leveled against architects of such a program: insensitivity to the feelings of those who are led to perceive themselves as outsiders to be 'assimilated' into the dominant culture and who resent this, or are psychologically harmed by the implication of cultural inferiority." He belittled the White men who developed these curricula: "The university teaching profession is almost entirely composed of academic achievers—mostly White and mostly male—who are steeped in the cultural lore in which they got their first high marks when they were school children. As the years pass in academe, it becomes increasingly difficult for them to liberate themselves from the conceptual world in which they have found much mutual reinforcement."[42]

Later in the semester, the same newspaper published an essay by a first-year student. This student argued that the WC requirement was "not only . . . a racist establishment, [it was also] a continuation of an ignorance that must be eradicated."The ignorance mentioned here was failing to acknowledge European colonialism, which "came over to the American continent, massacred the Indians, and introduced a well-established slave trade onto its fresh soil."The writer railed against the forced cultural assimilation of Native peoples in the face of European invasion and further objected to notions that only European culture has produced artifacts of value. The writer suggested that "Aristotle had some interesting ideas, but stimulating ideas have also been put forth by Africans, Asians, Latin Americans, and countless others from non-European backgrounds." The writer then suggested that a change to the WC program to more fully integrate minority perspectives would be a welcome panacea to persistent racism in America:

> Racism is very much alive in this world, and it is a problem that influ-
> ences the lives of everyone. If one wishes to solve this problem, one
> must understand it. I know all too well the ideals put forth by White
> America, but does White America understand the motivation behind
> Black America? . . . Our U.S. educational system is certainly not work-
> ing to dissolve this ignorance. . . . I find it disgusting that this "great"
> nation of ours honors people who enslaved other human beings. Men
> such as these practiced an evil and there is no excuse for evil. . . . The
> Western Culture program is an evil that denies many students the
> right to learn about their own cultures. I get sick and tired of my race
> being talked about only in the context of slavery. I get tired of reading
> the thoughts of White men who probably would spit on me if they
> were alive to face me today.[43]

There were already proposals for replacements of the WC program, though there had not been any word from curricular bodies that such a change might be desired. Two documents detail suggestions made by the BSU in the spring of 1986. In a memo from the BSU to the C-US, the BSU wrote that the current WC program had a "fundamental flaw" for its "failure to acknowledge the contributions and impact of women and people of color on [Western culture]." They called for "immediate redress" of the problem by creating an "American Cultures" track for implementation in the spring of 1990 (the WC program had eight different "tracks," year-long sequences that would fulfill the WC requirement). Such a track would examine "the culture, history, and contributions of people of color, women, and working-class people. Rather than being a permanent solution, this new track will serve as the first step towards a program encompassing the contributions of cultures disregarded and/or distorted by the present program." The memo stated that they made this request "with the support of President Donald Kennedy and Associate Dean of Humanities and Sciences, Carolyn Lougee." Furthermore, though the memo came from the BSU, the list of signatories included nine other individuals and five different extracurricular groups devoted to Black life on campus.[44]

It is clear in retrospect that this this debate over the curriculum was going to get ugly. For one, the memo sent by the BSU to the C-US was overly broad in its description of the current WC program, to the point of inaccuracy. Although it claimed that the WC program ignored the contributions of minorities, another memo circulated shortly after this substantially complicated the BSU narrative. Authored by Barry Katz, an instructor in the "Values, Technology, Science and Society" track of the current WC program, and John Perry, a professor of philosophy who also taught in the WC program—both of whom were vocally and historically supportive of bringing minorities into the record of Western civilization—called criticisms like those made by the BSU "uninformed and irresponsible." They suggested that such criticism was alienating many people in the WC program who were sympathetic to minority students' concerns and already actively working to address them. The authors acknowledged that changes did need to be made to the program as a whole but that descriptions of the program in the statements of its most passionate critics offered a caricature. They wished to establish more nuanced and accurate points about the program, particularly that

> the Western Culture Program was not conceived as, and does not exist as a celebration of Western Culture in the service of rationalizing the dominant establishment group of our own age and time, an

educational fossil from another age, or a device for diverting attention from racism and sexism. The facts are exactly the opposite. The program was intended to promote among Stanford students a more critical and reflective attitude toward the ideas and institutions that dominate our culture and has done so. Stanford faculty who have been attracted to participate, and especially the lecturers and instructors who have enriched the Stanford community as a result of the program, are as far as one could be from a cadre of establishment apologists, and they certainly deserve far better from the critics of the program than such a characterization.

Katz and Perry then suggested a point that would be reiterated often over the next two years of debate: that it is was a mistake to focus on just the WC program because it was a fairly small part of the students' overall general education at Stanford. They wrote that, in spite of criticisms of the program to which they were wholly sympathetic, they believed the school should retain a WC program because

> the ideas, good and bad, that were developed in this culture shape the ideological and institutional context of the lives of Stanford students more directly than those developed in other cultures. And, partly for this reason, these ideas and institutions are more easily grasped by beginning students than others that are less familiar. Finally because of the economic and military dominance of the West, there are few problems that the world faces whose understanding does not require some grasp of the ideas and institutions of the West, and in all such cases understanding will be helped if the understanding of those ideas and institutions is critical. These facts make the choice of Western Culture as the focus of an introductory required course quite reasonable.[45]

At the same time, there was an idea circulating that an individual course could be developed for the spring of 1987 that would deal with minority issues. Students could elect to take this course in the third quarter of the year, as a substitute for the third quarter of the track they were on for the first two quarters. Three proposals for such a class were made. One was offered by the BSU and endorsed by seven faculty members sympathetic to their proposal. Their suggestion was to simply import a class already extant at San Francisco State University titled "History of Racial and Ethnic Minorities: Comparative Analysis." The syllabus the BSU included in their proposal describes the course as having three objectives. First, the course sought to "examine to which extent the consequences of racial and cultural domination of African-Americans, Asian-Americans, La Raza, and Native American Indians were related to each other. . . . The first objective of the course is to help understand the causal structural characteristic of the domination (of US racial and ethnic minorities) which not only involved but transcended race." Second, the course aimed to "analyze and discuss the determinants and consequences of inequality in the distribution of power and privileges among US racial and ethnic minorities." Third, the course would "provide insight into the factors which give rise to racism and its role in the thwarting of economic interest of US racial and ethnic minorities and their responses to the institutional arrangements that structure their life opportunities."[46]

Still another proposal for a new spring course was offered by Sylvia Wynter, acting chair of the Department of African and Afro American Studies. Wynter titled the proposal "A Preliminary Proposal for an Alternative to the Present Core Curriculum Requirements." She called the course itself "American Synthesis: Toward an Alternative, Integrative Core Curriculum." Such a course might analyze the "ethnocultural and religious pluralism as well as the shared commonalities of the existential (i.e. lived) North American experience." The course would then use this perspective "to examine the adequacy of the present [WC program] as an integrative mechanism for our complex civilization," a civilization that is "unique in human history in that its emerging existential 'culture' is not isomorphic with this or that racial or ethnic group."[47]

The third proposal came from Clayborne Carson of the History Department. Carson would be a member of an "Area One Task Force" assembled a few months later that would propose and ultimately shepherd through changes to the WC that shaped the 1987 controversy. Further, his class was the one ultimately offered in the spring of 1987 as a third-quarter alternative to the existing WC tracks. The original title he proposed was "Western Culture and Its Victims"; however, the class actually offered was titled "Western Culture: An Alternative View." The historical record does not offer a reason for this change, but it was most likely the result of a suggestion during the course approval process. Carson's course was meant to be the alternative third-quarter track of the existing three-quarter sequence titled "Conflict and Change in Western Culture." This course would "stress the perspectives of individuals who have experienced Western cultural domination during the past two centuries." Further, the course would "depart from . . . the traditional emphasis on elite thought that has characterized most previous Western Culture courses. It will instead emphasize the critiques of dominant ideas produced by and on behalf of member of subordinate groups—especially poor people, racial minorities, and women—in Western societies."[48]

In the spring of 1986, the BSU reiterated their request to "replace [the] current Western Culture tracks with ones that include the historical and philosophical contributions of women and minorities." The BSU asked that the incoming class of 1990 have an "American Culture track that would emphasize 'the contributions of cultures disregarded and/or distorted by the present program.'" Further, the BSU was hoping for total replacement of the current WC program with a "world studies program, encompassing Africa, Europe, Asia, and the Americas."[49] The Associated Students of Stanford University, the main student governing body of the university, supported the implementation of the BSU's third-quarter course and a proposal for "a completely new World Culture Program" to replace the current WC program.[50]

The efforts of Dean Lougee, the BSU, and many others unnamed here paid off insofar as they resulted in a campus-wide forum on May 21, 1986, that was meant to explore the concerns expressed by members of the Stanford community about the current WC program. Titled "Western Culture: Education or Miseducation" in advertising flyers, Lougee in the *Stanford Daily* described the event as "a forum on Western Culture [that] will address issues of general interest to undergraduates and faculty."[51] In this article, Lougee noted that the faculty senate had asked for a report on the WC program and that the C-US had promised to furnish such a report after carefully considering the matters at hand. The day before the forum, Donald Kennedy suggested on a campus radio program that he was quite open to the criticisms being made and supportive of changes that might be made after the proper curricular and legislative bodies had thoroughly examined the issues.

An article published a few weeks after the forum shows that it was largely successful for those leveling criticisms about the program regarding the representation of women and minorities. At the May 21 meeting, the C-US called for a taskforce to be appointed "to undertake a comprehensive review of the Western culture program during 1986–1987," which Lougee and Provost James Rosse would begin building in June. On June 3, the C-US "endorsed the concept and development of a third-quarter Western Culture option, open to students from all tracks, which incorporates the experiences and cultural contributions of minorities and women."[52] This option was Clayborne Carson's course on an alternative view of Western culture. The C-US even took the highly unusual step of approving the offer of a course without having examined the syllabus, reading list, or other materials that might make up such a course prior to recommendation for approval by the senate. Apparently attuned to the tension and possible vitriol raised by the issues at hand, the dean of undergraduate studies said, "The [WC] program is now in its sixth year . . . a good time to look at where we are and where we are going—in a friendly way."[53]

However, as would be expected of such an endeavor, some were unhappy with the outcome of the meeting. The student president of the BSU was one dissatisfied attendee. In response to the chair of C-US calling for a taskforce to "determine in detail how to meet the legitimate concerns that have been raised among our faculty and students," the student president of the BSU said that she was "personally 'concerned and disturbed' by the recommendation because it did not mention BSU's proposals calling for the gradual implementation of the world culture program."[54] A student letter penned by an undeclared sophomore who attended the forum said that he was "struck by the number of times the term 'White male oppression' was used to describe the admittedly large number of White male thinkers read in Western Culture. I would only suggest to those who read Kafka, Nietzsche, and Marx (White male thinkers all) in their Western Culture classes to think again. . . . The majority of authors we read in Western Culture are engaged in self-examination and criticism of their predecessors, and we should not overlook this fact in the flurry of rhetoric about 'oppression' 'racism' and other quite legitimate charges we have heard recently."[55]

A professor of French, Robert Greer Cohn, published an essay in the *Campus Report* after the forum in which he stated his concerns that the energy for changes was coming mostly from students and how the proposed changes would abandon standards of aesthetic judgment. In a series of ill-chosen metaphors, Cohn said, "If an untutored beginner came among a group of basketball players and said 'You are excluding me; I am less expert than you; change the rules so I can play,' what would they say? So far the high game of Western culture (I do not say history) has been played by mostly European males, gracefully, expertly. And certain minority voices yell 'Not fair.'" Cohn then faulted the university at large for the lack of critical ability in its students. He wrote,

> The main reasons for our unsureness [of what constitutes "excellence" in cultural production] on this campus in these matters is that our University does *not* care enough, does not take the humanities very seriously and has played progressive (liberal) political games with them. Standards have been lowered even in the sciences, of late, but less so and less permanently. . . . But the humanities, here as elsewhere, were more open, because of the greater subjective component, to the replacement of masterpieces with works of minor ideologues or trendy figures, the choices of feminists and the like, a pandering to popular fads and campus revolutionaries. One of the most disappointing aspects of recent years has been the sellout of the dominant groups in academic power, letting their supreme heritage largely go to the dogs.

Cohn ended his letter with an accusation that anticipated the vitriol that would characterize the next few years, on both sides: "When perspectiveless young people abetted by resentful faculty threaten to pull down all the millennial strength and beauty on the page, score, canvas, by boycotting required classes that teach them, the proper answer is roughly the one you'd get from the basketball players."[56]

It is important to pause here, before getting into the heat of the battle, to highlight an important point that previous accounts of the canon wars so far have gotten wrong. Virtually no one on record in the archive was against the ends under discussion here (Cohn might be the singular exception)—that of bringing minorities into historical and educational enterprises. In the histrionics of the 1980s and 1990s, those who were critical of the work of this academic Left were often charged with being sexist, racist, and hellbent on keeping women and minorities out of history and education. As regards the Stanford episode, this could not be further from the truth. Everyone involved in this debate was working toward the same end—increasing the representation of minorities in the general education of Stanford students. The main arguments that commanded so much attention in the press concerned primarily the means by which this reform would happen; they were not arguments against it happening.

Over the summer of 1986, the taskforce that would consider changes to the WC program was assembled. Called the Area One Task Force (A1TF), it was ready to start work early in the fall quarter. In the archival materials that describe the formation of the taskforce, it is clear that a misunderstanding, perhaps catastrophic, was developing. In a memo to Carolyn Lougee, faculty member Ron Rebholz suggested that the committee seemed to be proceeding from a forgone conclusion that changes would be made, a suggestion he thought premature. He urged the committee to first examine the success of the current WC program before concluding that changes should be made. He also noted some growing tensions when he said of a letter he enclosed with his memo that "[the letter] confirms what I have been hearing from a lot of people since our recommendations, Martin Evans and John Perry being the most vocal, but there have been others: our recommendations have slapped the faces of people who have been trying to incorporate more material on minorities and women."[57] Further, the establishment of the taskforce had confused bureaucratic processes. The Western Culture Program Committee (WCPC) had already agreed to meet and discuss changes to the program in light of the criticisms being made about its inclusion of women and minorities. One email (Stanford was using a very primitive email system in June 1986) suggests that there was confusion in the charge of the taskforce because, "given the language you [Lougee] quoted in your text [a memo to various people requesting input as to the duties and composition of the A1TF] the justification for the Task Force is mighty redundant with a WCPC responsibility." Further, this writer stated that the WCPC could be expected to do a good job with its new chair, Paul Robinson, in conducting "serious review and reform of its programs, core lists, approaches, etc." The author also noted that the taskforce's job should be to determine "whether WCP (as good as can be made) should be THE means . . . of satisfying the three-quarter area one requirement."[58] Another colleague, Professor of History James Sheehan, suggested in a memo to Lougee that the criticisms leading to the formation of the ArTF were "intellectually slovenly." Sheehan did not "believe that the points raised against [the WC program] provide the basis for a thoughtful reconsideration of the course. If there is to be change, let it come in due time and after proper consideration, not as the hurried response to political pressures and ill informed protests."[59] Two female faculty members, Jane F. Collier and Sylvia Janagisako, members of the Feminist Studies Program Committee, wrote to the provost in July 1986 with concerns that women's issues were not adequately being represented in the debate over the WC requirement. They worried that "articles in the newspapers about the reevaluation of the Western Culture requirement have tended to focus on the concerns of ethnic and racial minorities. We do not want the concerns of women to be forgotten." Further, they requested that "a consideration of gender [be] integrated into all aspects of the program. The men who are seen as major contributors to the development of Western Culture made their contributions as men, not as genderless humans. A feminist perspective, properly integrated, can help freshmen to appreciate the role of gender relations as well as of ethnic and racial relations in shaping our shared cultural heritage."[60]

The ArTF got to work right away in the fall of 1986. Their charge from the C-US was to "undertake a comprehensive review in 1986–87 of the Western Culture Program as the means of satisfying Area One of the Distribution requirements." More specifically, the provost, James Rosse, asked the committee to do the following:

- Review the purposes, expectations, and assumptions underlying the current requirement
- Consider the extent to which the Western Culture Program has succeeded in meeting those purposes
- Determine whether or not the purposes, expectations, and assumptions underlying the current requirement should be changed in light of the legitimate concerns raised among our faculty and students, to which CUS refers
- Determine whether or not the courses that satisfy the requirement in the future should differ from those that currently satisfy it

- [If the previous question was answered in the affirmative] recommend the nature of those differences [and suggest] alternative course models that incorporate the changes.[61]

Rosse requested that the taskforce consult as widely as possible with
stakeholders, including the current WCPC and student and faculty
groups that had been lodging complaints.

Once the 1986–1987 school year got underway, interested student
groups had a lot to say about the taskforce. In a document titled
"Students' Charge to the Western Culture Task Force" dated August
1986 and written on behalf of the Third World community and the
women's community at Stanford, this document lays out their ideas
about the objectives of the taskforce. The letter suggests that the
AᴛTF would "examine the impact of the Western culture program on
undergraduates lives at Stanford," "determine what impact is desirable," and "determine what changes need to be made to the program
to produce the desired impact."[62] At the beginning of the academic
year, members of the BSU sent their thoughts and suggestions to the
nascent AᴛTF. They recommended "that the task force report on the
weaknesses of the Program." They "charged" the AᴛTF with developing "an alternative program to the current one that examines America
in the context of a global society, includes the experiences of people
of color in the U.S. and in their countries of origin, includes the experiences of women of all races, and includes class and the class inter-
action present in each culture." Further, the BSU offered some ideas
about the composition of the committee. They wrote that "given the
grievous oversights by the last Faculty Senate task force, we recommend that the new task force be composed by at least: 50% women,
50% Third World members, and two students."[63] In an escalation
of the criticism White men had recently received, in the eyes of the
BSU, White men should be categorically forbidden from sitting on
the committee.

The task force got right to work. In the archive there are several
Area One proposals that attempt to respond to the criticism of the
program. One, by chair of the AᴛTF, Paul Seaver, titled "The Origins of Contemporary Society and Culture," suggests an Area One
sequence that was chronological, had discussion sessions, used

primary texts, balanced "elite" and "non-elite" texts, and did not exclude texts by women or minority authors.[64] Another proposal by John Perry titled "First Year European Intellectual History" also valued small discussion sections, the use of primary texts, "classic works," and "significant attention paid to women, minorities, and other cultures." This plan further suggested that the course(s) should be "critical and analytical in tone, rather than celebratory."[65] Still another proposal, author unknown, suggested a sequence that also sought to use "primary works of significant intellectual merit" and a variety of genres of text—"literary, philosophical, political, poetic, historical." This scheme did not seek to retain the focus on "the West" because, it argued, "the West is already a problematical construct, and there is no reason arbitrarily to limit the field from which tracks may select their texts in this manner. A work of Indian philosophy, Chinese technology or African folklore may prove more consistent with the specific intellectual/pedagogic purposes of the track than one of the Great Books." Further, this author suggested that three new "tracks" merited development. They were "Gender and Culture," "Western and Non-Western Cultures," and "World Culture and the Americas." The proposal ends by suggesting that the criteria being developed to include minorities and women should be imposed on all tracks but the writer did not wish to impose "ideological uniformity" on the program.[66] History professor Clay Carson agreed that the new tracks should have a chronological structure, use primary texts, and have discussion sections. He also said that "while the particular balance of elite and non-elite texts, of dominant and subordinate, majority and minority voices can depend on the focus of the track, all should confront race, class, and gender; should examine cultural contact, and inter-action, and should include a substantial number of texts by women and non-White minorities."[67] This "confrontation" of "race, class, and gender" represented the ideology of identity politics reduced down to a pedagogically oriented package that would soon become dominant in humanistic and social scientific research and teaching. The requirement of an interpretive paradigm that "confronts" race, class, and gender in a universally required undergraduate sequence would seem to be exactly the type of ideological imposition one program proposal warned against.

Almost immediately there was confusion and slight alarm over what the ArTF was doing. This discomfort concerned the speed with which the committee was working. The charge from Provost Rosse in September had asked it to determine the extent to which the current WC program met new requirements the taskforce was developing. The taskforce seems to have skipped this step. But there was confusion too in the timeline that Rosse set out in September. Essentially, it was impossible from the start to both accomplish the tasks that Rosse charged the ArTF with and obey the timeline for the taskforce's work that Rosse had established. This confusion was evident by February 1987. At that time, the chair of the C-US, Marsh McCall, sent Paul Seaver, chair of the ArTF, a letter. It asked why the committee planned to have their work done in a few months, before the outcome of Clay Carson's course was known and before the review of the current WC program was completed. McCall was under the impression that the ArTF would be working for at least another year and sought to understand how he could have so misunderstood the situation.[68] Seaver's response was that he was finishing up in that amount of time because that was the charge from the provost. In this exchange of letters, it becomes clear that the C-US and many faculty did not think there was a problem with the current WC program and did not want it changed. Further, the ArTF thought that there had been a request for change in the C-US call for study the previous spring.[69]

The ArTF decided to release a draft of the proposal in April of 1987 entitled "Cultures, Ideas, and Values." It suggested that Stanford's liberal education should "include study of the cultural diversity that has become the heritage of us all." It implied that such study should be comparative, emphasize the global community that Stanford students are a part of, and view the United States as a multicultural society. More specifically, the objectives of the program would be

a) to broaden students' understanding of different cultures, cultural diversity, and the processes of cultural interaction both within a single culture and between different cultures;

b) to engage students with works that have intellectual impor-
   tance by virtue of the ideas they express, their mode of
   expression, or their influence;

c) to develop students' abilities to understand ideas and values,
   for the sake of self-understanding and understanding of
   others;

d) to enable students to increase their skills—in understanding
   and analyzing works, in reasoning and arguing for or against
   and interpretation, and in expressing their self-understanding
   and interpretation orally and in writing—and to prepare
   them for advanced work in the humanities, sciences, and
   engineering.

The proposed new program also had a diversity requirement. It suggested that year-long sequences that met the Area One requirement
must address diversity in three ways:

a) (geographical) to study at least one culture inside and at least
   one outside the European family of cultures. Each culture
   shall be treated on its own terms as well as in terms of its
   interactions with other cultures;

b) (historical) to have an historical dimension of at least five
   centuries. Students should become aware of the temporal
   relationship of works to each other and should understand
   some of the political, social, and economic contexts of the
   works;

c) (social) to confront issues relating to class, race, and gender,
   and to include a substantial number of works by women,
   minorities, and persons of color.[70]

The backlash against this proposal from the faculty was swift but
not universal. Those who supported the proposal as it was sent did
so for a few reasons. Some thought changes of this nature were long
overdue and that they would both bring needed flexibility to the

program and recognition of the talents of faculty who were trained in non-Western areas. These supporters also hoped the changes would encourage the hiring of more such faculty. Others disliked the arbitrary and sometimes incoherent nature of the "great works" focus of the current program and found the proposed changes to be a welcome departure from those shortcomings. Still others recognized that changes such as those proposed were in line with shifts already happening in the current WC program and that such a proposal would merely hasten them along.

A few responses to the proposal were mixed. One response from electrical engineering professor A. E. Seligman primarily had comments regarding the diversity requirement of the proposal. He was focused on the "social" diversity requirement that mandated engagement with issues related to race, class, and gender. He thought that the requirement was there "as an explicit statement, I think many would agree, because of its status as a currently active political issue." It was an objective he embraced, but he protested the requirement that stated "to include a substantial number of works by . . ." He found that phrase doubtful: "The number of works from any sources to be read in a given course should be dictated, one would think, by responsible judgment of the best way of meeting the objectives of the given course—not by a requirement that seems so blatantly political as this one."[71] Further, Seligman noted his surprise that religion did not appear anywhere in the draft, either as a matter of diversity or as a matter of studying at all. He thought this was an oversight. Others were generally in favor of the proposal but just thought it needed more detail.

Another professor, Van Harvey, of the Department of Religious Studies said that he thought the proposal suggested that "Area one should no longer be primarily concerned with whole [*sic*] sweep of 'Western Culture' but rather need only meet some minimal requirement of five centuries of 'European Culture' (in my view as equally an indeterminate entity as 'Western Culture')." Furthermore, he thought that the Area One requirement was meant to give all students a common understanding of a common intellectual history, a goal that was the basis for Area One being required and a reflection of a major, if largely unrealized, goal of general education for much of the twentieth century. He saw no reason to have the requirement if it did not foster some kind of shared intellectual experience among the students. He said he was further "disturbed" that the report had given the "nearly unanimous" impression to those currently involved in the program that they would henceforth be unqualified to teach in it. In the end, Harvey suggested clarifying whether the committee meant that the new program should teach "cultural diversity of the West (America?)" in the new program and not "cultural diversity as such."[72]

The faculty voices against this proposal were many and loud but not uncivil. Many faculty had concerns about the "comparative" requirements of the new proposal and about there being enough faculty qualified and willing to teach across cultures. There were also worries about the kind and amount of hiring that would need to be done to staff a new program. There were several concerns about the devaluation of primary texts and texts generally for a wider range of cultural artifacts. Several faculty members mentioned that the new proposal seemed to require an amount of coverage that was unreasonable for three quarters. A few noted that the problem at hand would be better dealt with by shoring up the already existing non-Western culture requirement in the general education program, rather than focusing on Area One.

The English Department was a vocal and unified voice against the proposal for a variety of reasons. Professor Ron Rebholz had fears that the program would no longer accommodate the teaching of the ancient world; that it imposed distinctly twentieth-century American concerns (diversity, multiculturalism, race, class, gender) on wide swaths of history that had no connections to such paradigms; and that the new requirement as proposed would be "a disaster for Area One."[73] Marjorie Perloff, a new faculty member in English, was deeply concerned by the "coerciveness" of the proposal. She saw the possibility of having "our classes policed in order to determine whether we are indeed towing the party line and teaching 'enough' women writers and/or minorities. The proposal reintroduces a proscriptiveness into the curriculum that I thought had gone out in the sixties."[74] The chair of the department, Al Gelpi, called the recommendations "disastrous because they blur the focus on Western Culture, make conscientious coverage from the ancient to the modern world impossible, and change the character of the course to so-called 'cultural history.'"[75]

The dean of humanities and sciences, Norman K. Wessells, while expressing support for cross-cultural sensitivity generally, did not believe it deserved the central place that putting it in Area One would give it. Further, he was worried about the rise of a "parafaculty" (what we would today call adjuncts or lecturers) to teach in this program rather than permanent faculty. Finally, he objected to the curriculum driving faculty and planning, saying that it would lead to a mediocre university.[76] Sylvia Wynter was concerned about the inherent tendency in Western culture to assume itself superior to other, non-Western cultures (what she called a hierarchical tendency). She hoped in this new program for means by which "the reciprocal recognition of cultural diversity must first be preceded by the conscious deconstruction of cultural heirachy [sic]." Wynter also worried that the proposal did not seem to require all students to study cultures different from their own. She stated,

> Whilst the Task Forces' recommendations place every emphasis on the need to study "cultures" not the student's own, i.e African, Asian, and Latin-American, it totally omits any mention of the need for all North American students to study those areas of the culture of North American civilization which are even more intellectually foreign to mainstream American students than are of Africa, Asia, Latin America. These areas are Native American, Afro-Black American, Chicano/Hispanic-American, Asian-American and to a lesser extent, Women's areas—that is all those areas who had to fight their way into academia in the Sixties—and to fight since then, to maintain a scandalously under-funded and precarious existence.[77]

The Stanford American Indian Organization objected to their group not being mentioned in the proposal as one to be studied under the new requirements for diversity.[78] More than a few faculty read the proposal as suggesting a program examining the idea of cultural diversity, as such, which few seemed to care for.

In a letter on behalf of the WCPC, Chair Paul Robinson conveyed the sentiments expressed by the committee at a recent meeting to discuss the proposal, feelings which "ranged from outrage to something considerably stronger than mild disappointment."[79] The letter suggests that the new proposal did not really address race, class, or gender, and Robinson regretted that the ArTF did not take into account efforts already underway in the WC program to address such issues. Robinson said the committee also wanted to retain some semblance of a core list focused on primary texts and was disappointed to see changes suggested in those areas.

Early in the 1987–1988 academic year, the proposal was still under revision. The ArTF was working to get the proposal to a version that the C-US could recommend unequivocally to the full senate for a formal vote. In one document compiled in October 1987, the chairs of the ArTF sent to the committee for consideration a list of changes to the proposal suggested by student groups such as the student senate; the BSU; MEChA, a Chican@/Latin@ advocacy group; the Asian American Student Association; and Students United for a Democratic Education. These groups requested more student representation on the steering committee for the new program, evaluation of the program every other year, and assurances there were equal numbers of European and non-European experts teaching in the program.[80] In a letter to the Stanford community confirming the rationale of a move away from a focus on the West in this new program, the chair of the BSU explained the group's position on the revision of the WC program at this point in time. They felt the program was "implicitly Eurocentric and biased." Consequently, "it is not enough to be critical of traditional perspectives, new perspectives are also required."[81]

C-US's response to the October changes to the document suggest that they were trying to dampen the activism and negative judgment they detected in ArTF's legislation. The C-US asked first that the committee remove and submit as a separate report to the senate an introductory "rationale" in the legislation. The committee suggested that the rationale would be useful to contextualize the legislation but that "we should not try to get Senate approval on what are basically ideological positions." The C-US also requested a revision of the language in a paragraph to be "less negatively judgmental. The paragraph suggests that the texts on the core list are taught uncritically; there are many faculty members who will take issue with this assumption." They asked to add an additional "objective" to the program, one written by a Professor Guerard who wanted "to encourage the experience of imaginative literature (novels, poems, plays) as a source of life-time pleasure in form and language, and as a means of enhancing the capacity to respond emotionally as well as intellectually to political, psychological, and moral ambiguity, and to the passions, conflicts, and choices of lives very different from our own." The C-US letter asked the AₜTF to "omit sentences beginning 'Parochialism comes in part. . . .' The committee believes these interpretive judgements are not necessary in the legislation." Finally, the C-US directly rejected two details suggested by the BSU regarding the number of students on the steering committee and the intervals of program review. It suggested the requests made by the BSU about composition of the steering committee were illegal under senate rules and that the intervals of program review the BSU wanted would place an unfair hardship on those conducting reviews.[82]

This letter and other documents in the archive indicate that there was still in the winter of 1987–1988 significant disagreement within the Stanford community regarding the new program. For example, Bill Chace, a leader in opposition to eliminating the West as a focus of the program, an advocate of retaining a "core list" and ensuring students had a common intellectual experience, wrote a letter with colleagues to the academic council dated January 11, 1988, that suggested he and the group he led were going to present another proposal for a new Area One program.[83] Over the next few months, up to the March 31 vote, there was quite a bit of negotiation and compromise undertaken to ensure the AₜTF proposal would ultimately pass in the senate. The first of these alterations, the "Bratman-Lindenberger Proposal," named for the faculty who wrote it, suggested that coverage of the ancient and medieval world be mandated and not suggested as it currently was, while maintaining a central focus on the last six to eight centuries. They also requested a change to an item in the proposal. In the November 1987 draft, item 5d was verbatim a suggestion made by the BSU that concerned the ends toward which the program would be evaluated. The BSU recommendation was that tracks would be evaluated based on enrollment numbers, which would then inform a discussion about whether tracks would be continued or eliminated. The Bratman-Lindenberger proposal suggested that tracks be evaluated for the degree to which there was a common learning experience across tracks.[84]

Clayborne Carson offered a revision in early March that relieved the concerns of many who lamented the lack of an explicit statement about a mechanism to encourage a common learning experience throughout the program. He suggested a new statement that read, "After consultation with the faculty of existing and proposed tracts [*sic*], establish annually, beginning in November, 1988, a set of common elements—such as themes and exemplary works related to these themes—to be included in all tracts approved for the following year."[85]

The most significant amendments, though, and the ones that likely ensured the passage of the proposal for a new "Cultures, Ideas, and Values" (CIV) program, were made mere weeks before the vote. They came out of a meeting that Paul Robinson, the director of the WC program that the CIV program would replace, convened with all faculty who taught in the WC program. He wrote of a "highly divided straw vote" on the question of a core list of readings at the last senate meeting and of "sensing a need for a strong compromise that would enable a large majority of the Senators to support the new . . . CIV legislation." The compromises he offered were a result of "the deep desire of this body of humanists and social scientists to reach a workable compromise that will not leave our community sharply divided." The amendments would "provide the necessary guarantee . . . of a 'common intellectual experience' for all students enrolled in the program." The first was called the "Carson-Chace" amendment because Clayborne Carson and Bill Chace, two faculty that represented the opposite poles of opinion on what to do with Area One, wrote it. It replaced the instructional objective that tracks must "focus on primary works, written or otherwise, although secondary works may also be used . . . to give substantial attention to the issues of race, gender, and class during each academic quarter, with at least one of these issues addressed explicitly in at least one major reading in each quarter." Robinson said of this amendment that it meant "that all the tracks, would share at least three common themes . . . [which guarantees] a common intellectual experience in all the tracks."[86] This essentially replaced pedagogical goals with a particular interpretive lens;

it substituted a generic call for a primary text with the much more specific requirement of the interpretive framework of race, class, and gender, the pedagogical version of the identity politics developing throughout the decade.

The other amendment, written by Carson and Paul Seaver, was meant "to establish a process whereby all tracks would be assured of sharing further common elements." This item read, "[The Area One Program Committee shall] supervise an annual process by which the regular faculty and course coordinators who will be teaching in the various tracks will meet to discuss their syllabuses for the following year and to agree on those common elements—texts, authors, themes or issues—that will be taught by all the tracks." Robinson wanted to show the senate how the amendments would work, to further make the case for passage of the new program. He noted that his group had decided on common texts for the 1988–1989 school year, three of which "will be chosen to meet the common themes of race, class, and gender specified in the Carson-Chace amendment." Another six common texts would be "Plato, the Hebrew and Christian Bible, Augustine, Machiavelli, Rousseau, and Marx." Robinson was quick to distance his group from any charge that they took these works to be "great." Rather, "they are simply and pragmatically six common authors we could reach ready and virtually unanimous agreement on for next year's courses." He also noted that the group was moving away from a belief in the need for a "core list" and toward creating a "common intellectual experience."[87]

This last-minute politicking did what it was meant to do: a program titled "Cultures, Ideas, and Values" was voted in on March 31, 1988, to replace the WC program adopted in 1980 by a decisive vote of thirty-nine for, four against, and five abstaining.[88]

For all the sound and fury of the previous two years, the CIV program did not last long. It was replaced in 1997 by a course called "Introduction to the Humanities" (IHUM). I was unable to locate much to explain the pedagogical goals or approach of IHUM. What I could find said that it was a "one quarter introductory course taught by a team of faculty members in the fall quarter and a subsequent two-quarter thematic sequence in winter and spring quarters."[89] Further the switch to IHUM meant that students read fewer books, a metric that had been shrinking for thirty years. Reading lists had as many as fifteen books on them in the 1980s but not more than ten during the CIV days from 1988 to 1997. IHUM often had reading lists of just five books. IHUM lasted about fifteen years until it was replaced by "Thinking Matters" (TM) in 2012. TM courses were meant to offer students flexible and broad options for a general education lecture course in their first year. Further, the program allowed courses to come from "any field of study at the university, taught in any term, and adopt a variety of course sizes and meeting formats appropriate to their subject matter and goals." The TM program was made up of courses that were "organized around a major idea, question, or problem of general interest, rather than as introductory surveys of some disciplinary fields, and they should be oriented toward the needs of freshman learners."[90] In a sense, the TM program was a demotion for the humanities for two reasons: first, in IHUM the content of the program was presumably focused on humanities fields and thought; second, one of its most "significant aspects," according to Judy Goldstein, C-USP (formerly C-US) chair, was that while IHUM was administered solely by the School of Humanities and Sciences, the "responsibility for Thinking Matters [would] be spread across the university."[91]

In 2016, there was a return to the controversy of the late 1980s over what became CIV when the *Stanford Review*, a conservative, student-run newspaper started by Peter Thiel and a peer when they were students at Stanford, issued a "manifesto" named the "Western Civilization Ballot Initiative" that claimed, "It's time to revive Stanford's humanities core." This humanities core, the manifesto suggested, was meant to replace TM because "Stanford has fewer humanities requirements than any other elite college." It wanted the focus to be on Western civilization because "it underpins our society." The underpinnings the *Review* had in mind were "the development of industry, political rights, and globalization," an inquisitive nature, and a focus on individual rights.[92] There was swift and fierce backlash against this proposal. One Stanford student challenged the manifesto's claims of fostering inquiry and more freedom, saying that "such noble aspirations are inherently hampered by their position within a racist, sexist, and classist system which sought—and still seeks—to explicitly uphold White supremacy and the subjugation of all others."[93] Another student wrote an essay offering a point-by-point refutation of claims offered in the manifesto. This author concluded her essay by saying she was "deeply disturbed that some of my peers have the audacity to disrespect the Stanford community in such a way. To be fair, as many others have mentioned, I could get behind this if it were framed as understanding Western civilization in order to deconstruct it—that is understanding Western values so that we could better understand oppression and marginalization."[94] A few other student essays condemned the manifesto in similar terms.

This debate happened at the same time that humanities faculty were developing a new "Humanities Core," which was not a proposal for their general education program but rather a proposal to develop a non-required program that would offer any interested student "a structured and guided pathway into the humanities." It had four tiers: foundations, which "[focused] on the ancient origins of world civilizations"; traditions, which "[studied] the history and traditions of various cultures through a three course sequence"; disciplines, which "[was] comprised of introductory courses for various disciplines in the humanities"; and a fourth tier that was a "series of advanced seminars in the humanities." This humanities core was different from the general education programs "Structured Liberal Education" or "Education as Self-Fashioning" because those programs were offered only to first-year students, and the humanities core would be open to any undergraduate student who wanted to study the humanities. This newly proposed Humanities Core was adopted for implementation in the 2016–2017 school year. The *Stanford Review* considered the adoption of this core a victory because the core only included a "European, 'Great Books, Big Ideas' track" initially, though it was expected to expand in the near future to "other non-Western cultures."[95]

The TM program was still in place in 2019 when faculty decided they wanted to replace it with a first-year program "focusing on civic education and global citizenship."[96] The program was named COLLEGE, which stands for "Civic, Liberal, and Global Education." It was accepted by faculty and implemented for the 2022–2023 school year. The COLLEGE program will "help students discover 'what makes living worthwhile' while 'developing the skills that empower and enable us to live together.'"[97] The program's director, Dan

Edelstein, argues that what makes COLLEGE an improvement over TM is that it provides a "shared intellectual experience for all first year students." The COLLEGE program is a "three course sequence taught over three quarters." The fall course is called "Why College? Your Education and the Good Life," which is followed by a winter course titled "Citizenship in the 21st Century." The spring course is focused on global perspectives and is one of "8–12 thematic courses that take a multidisciplinary approach to questions of global concern. These spring courses focus on topics ranging from sustainability to gender and sexuality."[98] As of this writing, the COLLEGE program is in its first year. How it unfolds, its successes and failures—I am sure there will be many, including some in the national press, who are eager to see and evaluate its impact.

CHAPTER 4

THE ESCALATING CANON WARS AND RACISM AND SEXISM AT THE UNIVERSITY OF TEXAS, AUSTIN

CIV— CULTURES, IDEAS, VALUES: Allan Bloom, author of *The Closing of the American Mind*, an unexpected bestseller of 1987, would be horrified.[1] That text, along with the Western culture debate at Stanford, were two of the most visible and discussed instances of the general, albeit educated, public becoming aware of the effects of the curricular activism of college professors in the 1960s and 1970s. Over the next several years, there would be an explosion of newspaper, magazine, and scholarly articles and popular and academic books on political correctness, multiculturalism, illiberalism, and the radicalism that had been developing in academia since the 1960s. Feature articles in *Time, Newsweek*, and similar publications, along with books like Roger Kimball's *Tenured Radicals* (1990), Dinesh D'Souza's *Illiberal Education* (1991), and Richard Bernstein's *Dictatorship of Virtue* (1994), got wide media and academic coverage in the late 1980s and early 1990s.[2] Furthermore, this debate, which only in retrospect was named the canon wars, was quickly divided into liberal and conservative camps, a sort of academic manifestation of the larger culture wars. Some of this came from the relentless and nasty campaigns of GOP strategist Arthur Finkelstein to turn the word "liberal" into an epithet. Some of it came from radicalized academics who often saw any criticism of their beliefs as part of a conservative conspiracy that was hostile to Leftist thought in general. However, the heated public reaction to the changes Left and Left-learning

academics had wrought on education since the 1960s is really better understood as a conflict between classical liberals and a radical
academic Left (a distinction that is all but extinct today, based on the
media's frequent labeling of far Leftist activism as "liberal") about
the impact of curricular activism on education and, consequently, on
American society.

At the time it was published, Bloom's book was hailed or hated,
depending on one's political leanings, as a conservative commentary
on the impact of the academic Left on intellectual life in America.
Such a judgment suggests the book was perhaps more bought than
read, however, because Bloom's work is fundamentally an indictment
of relativism, drawn with a rather broad brush. He argued that as a
culture we no longer think in absolutes (e.g., good versus evil) but
with relative criteria (e.g., values, lifestyle). The common use of the
term "values" as a way of discussing moral life is an indication of
the relativism Bloom reviled. He believed that it was essential for a
human society to have preferences and to separate out the good, the
bad, and the ugly in human endeavors—social organizations, artistic production, morality, and so on—and he grounded this belief in
a canonical understanding of classical and Enlightenment political
theory. He also claimed that the turn toward relativism and away
from a hierarchical society with a "dominant" class who sets the rules
of morality, taste, and social organization is the result of a development in liberalism toward "openness." The openness he indicted is
the process by which America in the twentieth century extended
rights, respect, and protection to groups like non-Caucasians, homosexuals, women, and children, who were previously excluded from
such privileges—a process Richard Rorty described elsewhere as the
diminishment of "socially accepted sadism."[3]

Bloom was likely unopposed to the disappearance of socially
accepted sadism; his quarrel was with *how* it happened: via unwashed
masses using historicist methods and Marxist ideology rather than
by a social elite appealing to the natural rights doctrine of Enlightenment political philosophy and America's founding documents. Social
changes brought by Marxism, historicism, and the masses were,
Bloom claimed, a *closing*, not an opening, of the American mind
because historicism especially "remove[s] the authority of men's

reason" and promotes the belief that "all thought is essentially related to and cannot transcend its own time." Methods like historicism diminish curiosity and the quest for knowledge, he believed. Bloom explained that there is a type of openness that is really closedness, an "openness of indifference—promoted with the twin purposes of humbling our intellectual pride and letting us be whatever we want to be, just as long as we don't want to be knowers." The other kind of openness, real openness according to Bloom, "invites us to the quest for knowledge and certitude, for which history and the various cultures provide a brilliant array of examples for examination. This second kind of openness encourages the desire that animates and makes interesting every serious student."[4]

The vast majority of the book is an intellectual history of the origins of our relativist culture, which Bloom blamed on academics' embrace of Nietzsche in Western political and economic thought. He also lamented, at some length, an ideal that was never fulfilled: the ideal promised by a Great Books tradition. Bloom described early in the book his belief in "the real motive of education, the search for a good life." Such an education should, according to Bloom, explore "great questions that must be faced if one is to live a serious life: reason-revelation, freedom-necessity, democracy-aristocracy, good-evil, body-soul, self-other, city-man, eternity-time, being-nothing." Bloom made a poignant case for the value that such an education had for him at the University of Chicago in the 1940s but also seemed to understand that such an education was a largely unrealized ideal in American universities.[5]

Whatever else the canon wars did—and they did a lot—this episode made routine bureaucratic work in American colleges and universities anything but routine. Just two years after the conflict over the Western culture program at Stanford that received so much local and national attention, another curricular battle appeared in the press, this time at the University of Texas, Austin. In the spring of 1990, a subcommittee of the English Department sought to revise the curriculum of ENG 306, a universally required written composition course that many felt had become unfocused and unproductive. One of the issues the committee faced was a common one for this kind of class both then and now: the question of what kind of content or topics a class that is essentially about writing skills should use. At the time, and to some extent now, the dominant content for the class at UT Austin was a compilation of literary reading, usually literary essays that students could use. Exactly how students use such texts to further their writing skills is a matter of some debate and doubt, but it seems that in this case, the students were expected to see such essays as models for their own compositions.

By the spring of 1990, this approach to ENG 306 was found wanting for a number of reasons, and the committee set out to give the class some valuable content that students could write about, thus creating a more robust and focused experience. They also sought to standardize to some degree what was happening across dozens of sections serving some three thousand students, an improvement in the cohesion of the entire program. The committee decided that the class would now focus on exploring the idea of "difference," and it would get at such knowledge via a sociology textbook called *Racism and Sexism* by Paula Rothenberg. The class would also get at this concept of "difference" by examining "various U. S. Supreme Court decisions on racial and sexual discrimination."[6] This change was reported by the local Austin newspaper, the *Austin American-Statesman*. In late May and in the summer of 1990, this change to ENG 306 was litigated in the local and national press, though not to the degree that the debate over the core at Stanford was a few years earlier. A rather histrionic letter to the editor penned by another UT English professor, Alan Gribben, claimed that ENG 306 had "fallen prey to the current mania for converting every academic subject into a politicized study of race, class, and gender."[7] Gribben thought that a class such as the one proposed would result in students "having their social attitudes as well as their essays graded by English Department instructors in what has to be the most massive effort at thought-control ever attempted on the campus."[8] He concluded his letter by suggesting that if the course was to be politicized in the manner proposed, the state legislature would be justified in canceling it. The next day, the *New York Times*, ever attentive to campus life at elite schools, reported on the controversy. This article described recent unrest on UT Austin's campus as "racial" and resulting in the suspension of two fraternities, and speculated that the changes to ENG 306 might be a response to that. In this article, another UT English professor who was on the ENG 306 committee, John Ruszkiewicz, voted against the proposal to change ENG 306 because he believed that the *Racism and Sexism* text was a work demonstrating "'a far-Left view with no countervailing opinion." Linda Broadkey, the chair of the ENG 306 committee and an advocate for the changes proposed, was somewhat on the defensive. She told the *New York Times* that she would ensure the course did not indoctrinate students and that she had made clear to the graduate students who would be teaching the course that "it is not a course in identity politics."[9]

In late July 1990, the *Austin American-Statesman* reported that Standish Meacham, the dean of the College of Liberal Arts at UT Austin, had decided to postpone the implementation of the class by one year—to the fall of 1991—a mere six weeks before it was to begin. Meacham made this decision based on the concerns raised both within and outside of Austin's campus about the politicization of the course. The newspaper reported that the proposed class had divided both the English Department committee working on the problem and other faculty on campus. The *Racism and Sexism* text had been thrown out because its subject matter was too narrow; two committee members had resigned over the proposed changes, accusing other committee members of "working in secret"; and fifty-six faculty from around campus had signed an open letter in the campus newspaper, the *Daily Texan*, opposing the changes.[10]

In late August, one of the professors who had resigned from the ENG 306 committee, James Duban, wrote an editorial in the *Austin American-Statesman* objecting to the new ENG 306 on pedagogical grounds. Duban believed that the focus of a written composition class should be "the perfecting of basic writing skills," and that "various topics (including social ones) that motivate students to write should only receive passing attention from the instructor." Further, he was concerned that the new proposed class would make "the discussion and researching of social, political, and legal topics" the "defacto subject matter" of the one required composition class at the university.[11]

The question raised by Duban is a common one in this type of course. The disagreements over whether written composition should be a class with subject matter content, or a class where the content is a focus on abstract writing and revising skills, is a matter that has plagued such classes for decades and continues to do so. In a reply editorial several days later, Broadkey and her colleague John Slatin responded to Duban with an *ad hominem* attack that was characteristic of the reaction of some radicalized academics to criticism. They wrote that professors like Alan Gribben and James Dugan "feel that the new syllabus represents an unprecedented 'politicization' of a course they evidently believe to have been politically neutral in the past—which simply means that previous syllabi embodied their political views." They agreed that writing should be the focus of a writing course but that topics about which students would write should "receive far more than 'passing attention from the instructor.'" Rather than following up that statement with an explanation of why topics in the composition course should receive attention, they inexplicably stated that "the topics for the course we had proposed to begin teaching on Aug. 29th come from the readings." Broadkey and Slatin then ended the editorial by writing that "Professor Duban says that ENG 306 should aim at 'perfecting basic skills.' That doesn't mean writing in a vacuum. It means perfecting the ability to write effective, well-argued essays about things that matter."[12] In a response to this editorial, Gribben wrote into the *Austin American-Statesman* again suggesting that Broadkey's defense of the class "conveniently" failed to mention the choice of *Racism and Sexism* as the required reader, a text that "portrays the United States as having completely failed women and people of color. The textbook implies that a Marxist class analysis of American society is essential for combating its evils." In response to the attacks Broadkey and Slatin had made against Duban previously, Gribben wrote that

the charge was made again in this recent column that I and others favor an impossible ideal—a politically neutral English course that in reality only reflects my own political views. Let us assume for a moment that all academic enterprises are ultimately political, as radicalized faculty in the humanities seem so fond of insisting these days. In that case, the political vision of the classroom that I can subscribe to is the one in which truly free debate is possible, in which balanced view of our society are supplied in the assigned readings, and in which instructors and students have some choices regarding topics and approaches.[13]

In January 1991, Maxine Hairston, a nationally recognized scholar of rhetoric and composition, the scholarly field that usually oversees written composition classes, weighed in on the revision to ENG 306. She noted that the plans to revise the class had blown up into a "national controversy" over whether the changes were a part of "a larger movement by the academic far Left to impose a 'politically correct' orthodoxy on colleges and universities nationwide." Hairston suggested that she thought such a judgement was "at least partially correct" but that she objected to the course changes on pedagogical grounds. Pedagogically, she believed a writing class should focus on using writing as a tool for discovering, organizing, and revising arguments, and it should teach logic and rhetoric to convey the students' thinking. She was concerned that the revised ENG 306, focused as it was on "politically charged social issues," could not achieve these goals. Further, she objected to supporters of the new ENG 306 characterizing opponents of the changes as "Right wing extremists without a social conscience."[14]

The national controversy seems to have broken the process of trying to revise ENG 306. In early February, the committee overseeing this task voted to disband and gave up their efforts. They composed a letter to the chair of the English Department, Joseph Kruppa, which "accus[ed] the administration of being indifferent to their efforts to revise the course" and suggested that the administration had caved to criticism raised in the national coverage of the controversy. Broadkey said that they voted to disband after they were unable to meet with the university president, William Cunningham, over the matter. In response, Cunningham issued a statement that emphasized "Texas's commitment to multicultural education." He said he had not supported the idea of running a pilot of the course in the spring of 1991 because there had not been enough open debate about the changes. He observed, "When a drastic change is being made to a required course, I think the rest of the faculty have a right to take part in the discussion and I don't think that process had been completed."[15] Further, it was reported that the department chair and the dean of the college had vocally supported the course and that there was suspicion that the dean "caved" because of pressure from the president.[16]

A controversy such as this has many casualties. Dean Meacham resigned from his deanship effective at the end of the spring term 1991.[17] The English Department lost at least three faculty: Alan Gribben resigned from his tenured professorship at the end of 1991; a year later in 1992 Broadkey left UT Austin for a position at the

University of California, San Diego. At the same time, James Duban left Austin for a position at the University of North Texas. The *Austin American-Statesman* reported that the new dean, Robert King, believed that Duban's departure was a casualty in a "war over political correctness."[18]

This "war over political correctness," Bloom's book *The Closing of the American Mind,* the controversy over Western culture at Stanford—we can think of these things as the early battles in a war of words regarding the impact of radical academics on American academia. As the episode at UT Austin was unfolding in 1990 and 1991, two books, ostensibly conservative, were receiving much media attention. The first was Roger Kimball's *Tenured Radicals,* which sought to outline and criticize the politicization of higher education. He suggested that "higher education has long been an important front in the culture war that began in the 1960's, a war whose aim is to remake American society according to a Left-wing antinomian blueprint." Still another claim he made is characteristic of criticism of academic radicals by those who are often taken to be conservative. He suggested that the recent curricular activism had caused

> nothing less than the destruction of the fundamental premises that underlie our conception of both liberal education and of a liberal democratic polity. Respect for rationality and the rights of the individual; a commitment to the ideals of disinterested criticism and color-blind justice; advancement, according to merit, not according to sex, race, or ethnic origin; these quintessentially Western ideas are bedrocks of our political as well as educational system. And they are precisely the ideas that are now under attack by politically correct academics intoxicated by the coercive possibilities of inherent in [*sic*] the ideology of virtue.[19]

The other high-profile book was Dinesh D'Souza's *Illiberal Education.* In this book, D'Souza argued that "an academic and cultural revolution is underway at American universities." Such a revolution had an effect, D'Souza claimed, on how students were admitted to college, how students funded their education, "what they learn and how they are taught." The recent curricular activism was also, according to D'Souza, changing campus life and what students could say and believe in those spaces. He quoted disapprovingly a statement by the University of Wisconsin chancellor Donna Shalala in which she claimed that "a basic transformation of American higher education in the name of multiculturalism and diversity" was currently taking place. D'Souza went on to suggest that this was a "victim's revolution" and was fought by campus liberals on behalf of "those who suffer from the effects of Western colonialism in the Third World, as well as race and gender discrimination in America."[20]

The episode at UT Austin appeared in several commentaries in the national media related to Kimball's and D'Souza's claims. The ever-satirical Jonathan Yardley wrote a letter to Santa in the Christmas Eve 1990 edition of the *Washington Post* that requested a travel ticket for "all those people who believe that the real purpose of education is political indoctrination." This ticket would take these people to Albania, "that socialist paradise" where "the government isn't big on free speech . . . but then, neither are the folks we're sending there." Specifically, Yardley targeted Stanley Fish of Duke University, those at UT Austin who were involved in developing "oppression English," and various English professors at the University of Massachusetts, Amherst.[21] Shortly after the publication of this satire, the *New York Times* covered the situation at Amherst about which Yardley wrote. The English faculty there, because of what happened at UT Austin, received attention for their efforts to "include issues of racial and social diversity in writing classes," though the faculty insisted they were teaching students how to write, not how to be politically correct. The director of the writing program, Anne Herrington, said that the changes were made to the program in 1988 after a "racially motivated brawl broke out on campus between White and Black students after the 1986 World Series. The university was 'consciousness-shocked' after the incident, in which one Black student was seriously injured." Herrington worried that "by failing to include a variety of writers and perspectives in the curriculum, 'we thought, my God, could we be contributing to this.'" Another faculty member, Marcia Curtis, the coordinator of basic writing (at this time, probably a remedial class for students whose writing skills were not yet at a level that would foster success in college), said that her program "tried very hard to include writers from various cultures so that students could see themselves as writers. . . . I don't want the kids to think that Black writers can only write about racism or that Jewish writers can only write about anti-Semitism or the Holocaust." Further, Herrington said that the college writing programs required "the 80 teaching assistants and 10 faculty members who teach the courses to participate in a three-day sensitivity training workshop help by a campus development trainer."[22]

By the spring of 1991, the effect of academic radicals on higher education was well-established and creating controversy everywhere. This was captured in a Sunday features article in the *Washington Post* titled "The Book Wars: Campuses Split over the New Multicultural Criteria." The title of the article pointed to the fact that identity politics married to undergraduate educational curricula was known by the early 1990s as multiculturalism. Multiculturalism here seems to have been a broad term that referred to a whole host of developments: the prominence that the new minority studies formed at the end of the 1960s had acquired by the 1990s; the use of race, class, and gender as paradigms of study in many undergraduate classes in the humanities and social sciences; and the general tendency of formerly unrepresented peoples demanding recognition in educational enterprises. The article described a summer study session at the University of Maryland in which scholars from a wide variety of fields met to "either transform the syllabus for one of their courses to take into account issues of race and gender or come up with an entirely new gender- and race-sensitive course in their field. (It should be noted that in this arena, gender no longer refers to grammar but to a broad spectrum of issues involving sexual roles, preference, and identity)." The article then explained how many such endeavors were underway across the country. In addition to the conflicts at Stanford and UT Austin, Judith Weinraub, the author, described how in 1990, "a seminar on the art of Northern Europe at Wellesley College considered 'a series of works dating from the 15th through the 20th centuries, in relation to contemporary notions regarding sex, gender, and power. The premise for our investigation of works by Van Eyck, Rubens, De Hooch, Watteau, Manet, and Picasso,' said the 1990 catalogue, in politically tinged academese, 'is that at a given historical moment, figurations and domestic relationships serve as paradigmatic expressions of political and economic beliefs.'" Weinraub also mentioned "a statewide curriculum transformation project funded by the New

Jersey Department of Education [that] seeks to encourage and support work that integrates 'issues of women and gender, race, class, ethnicity, homophobia and heterosexism' into the curriculum." Weinraub described a "cluster of attitudes" under a "multicultural umbrella" that are "lumped together as Left-wing and known as politically-correct or p.c.," which has "achieved a fashionable status that has transformed the college classrooms and the way people talk. In part, 'political correctness' is designed to make students think about the sex-role or racially insensitive assumptions inherent in language: freshmen have become 'frosh' or 'first-year students,' racial minorities, 'people of color.'"[23]

An avalanche had begun. The next few years would see hundreds of books, articles, and essays explaining, exploring, defending, and criticizing the curricular changes academic radicals had wrought. In 1992, an edited collection by Paul Berman, *Debating P.C.: The Controversy over Political Correctness on College Campuses*, brought together many well-known scholars and journalists to explore these controversies.[24] Michael Berube, now a distinguished professor at Penn State, decried the vilification in the public press of young literary scholars who were working within theoretical paradigms. He accused public critics of not actually reading the work of these scholars and aimed his vitriol at the *New Republic*, the *New York Times Book Review*, the *New York Review of Books*, and *Atlantic Monthly*, whose publication of Dinesh D'Souza's essay "Illiberal Education," a shorter version of the book, raised Berube's ire. Berube believed the fact that the *Atlantic Monthly* published the essay indicated "an important sign of the extent to which public discussion of American academia is now conducted by the most callow and opportunistic elements of the Right."[25] The late Edward Said contributed an essay to *Debating P.C.* illustrating the limits of scholarly work done in the paradigm of identity politics. He told of a recent experience participating in a seminar "at a historical studies center of a historically renowned American university." The paper he gave was the introduction to his work subsequent to *Orientalism*, which dealt "with the relationship between modern culture and imperialism" and described "the emergence of a global consciousness in Western knowledge at the end of the nineteenth century, particularly in such apparently unrelated fields as geography and comparative literature." He described his exchange with "a professor of history, a Black woman of some eminence who had recently come to the university but whose work was unfamiliar to me." Said explained that "she announced in advance that her question was to be hostile, 'a very hostile one in fact.' She then said something like the following: for the first thirteen pages of your paper, you talked only about White, European males. Thereafter on page 14 you mention some names of non-Europeans. 'How could you do such a thing?'" Said replied that he was "discussing European imperialism, which would not have been likely to include in its discourse the work of African-American women." Said then gave a long defense and explanation of his work in reply to this scholar's hostility, after which Said observed that when he finished,

> She did not proceed [with her question] and I was left to suppose that she considered her point sufficiently and conclusively made: I was guilty of not mentioning living, non-European nonmales, even when it was not obvious to me or, I later gathered, to many members of the seminar what their pertinence might have been. I noted to myself that my antagonist did not think it necessary to enumerate what specifically in the work of living non-Europeans I should have used, or which books and ideas by them she found important and relevant. All I had been given to work with was the asserted necessity to mention some approved names—what names did not really matter—as if the very act of uttering them was enough. I was also left unmistakably with the impression that as a non-White—a category incidentally to which as an Arab I myself belong—she was saying that to affirm the existence of non-European "others" took the place of evidence, argument, and discussion.[26]

A debate between Diane Ravitch and Molefi Kete Asante in Berman's collection, over multiculturalism in K–12 schools, illuminates how ugly some of these debates got. In her essay, Ravitch, as an education historian, affirmed the pluralistic nature of American history and supported efforts to change educational programs to reflect such a nature. But she suggested that recent "painstaking efforts to expand the understanding of American culture into a richer and more varied tapestry have taken a new turn, and not for the better." She made a distinction between pluralistic multiculturalism and particularistic multiculturalism. She wrote that pluralistic multiculturalism "seek[s] a richer common culture" but that particular multicultural-ists "insist that no common culture is possible or desirable." She saw this particularism entering the K–12 schools in "ethnocentric curri-cula" designed to "raise the self-esteem and academic achievement of children from racial and ethnic minority backgrounds. Without any evidence, they claim that children from minority backgrounds will do well in school *only* if they are immersed in a positive, pride-ful version of their ancestral culture. If children are of, for example, Fredonain ancestry, they must hear that Fredonians were important in mathematics, science, history, and literature." Ravitch found this particularistic multiculturalism

> unabashedly filiopietistic and deterministic. It teaches children that their identity is determined by their "cultural genes." That something in their blood or their race memory or their cultural DNA defines who they are and not what they may achieve. That the culture in which they live is not their own culture even though they were born here. That American culture is "Eurocentric" and therefore hostile to anyone whose ancestors are not European. Perhaps the most invidious impli-cation of particularism is that racial and ethnic minorities are not and should not try to be part of American culture.[27]

In Asante's response, he launched into a particularly ugly *ad homi-nem* attack that was, unfortunately, not infrequently so characteristic of Leftist academics' response to criticism. He began with a long dis-course on how scholars are always "implicated" in the arguments they make. He suggested that Ravitch's essay indicated her participation in a "neo-Aryan" model of history that was similar in spirit to the South African apartheid regime. He suspected a "mutual conspiracy" of which Ravitch was a part between "race doctrine and educational doctrine in America. Professor Ravitch and others would maintain the façade of reasonableness even in the face of arguments demon-strating the irrationality of both White supremacist ideas on race and White hegemonic ideas in education." He then accused her of being dishonest in her support of multiculturalism, which he believed was "nothing more than an attempt to apologize for White cultural supremacy in the curriculum by using the same logic as White racial supremacists used in trying to defend White racism in previous years."[28]

Finally, in 1994, a high-profile book by Richard Bernstein titled *Dictatorship of Virtue: How the Battle over Multiculturalism Is Reshaping Our Schools, Our Country, and Our Lives* argued that "the whole point of the liberal revolution that gave rise to the 1960's was to free us from somebody else's dogma, but now the very same people who fought for personal liberation a generation ago are striving to impose on others a secularized religion involving a set of values and codes that they believe in, disguising it behind innocuous labels like 'diversity training' and 'respect for difference.'" He further suggested that what he called a "dictatorship of virtue" also went by an "end of century designation," political correctness.[29]

Radicalized Leftist academics no doubt can be credited with many of the most positive social, political, and cultural developments of the last fifty years. The inclusion of women, non-Whites, homosexuals, genderqueers, and the differently abled in our social life and historical record is a feat long overdue and deeply woven in a short period of time, even if there is more work to do on inclusion. The merit of the ultimate ends toward which the academic Left worked is, without doubt, great and unshakable. Nevertheless, these radicalized academics can also be credited with some ill effects on our culture, arising from the means by which they sought their ends; such means ultimately, for all the good they did, also may have contributed to the virulent political polarization America experiences today, a claim which is explored next.

CONCLUSION

There are two dangers in political polarization, and they are related. The first is the lack of human understanding that such polarization brings: people are bludgeoned into being, either "us" or "them," and the realities of the human situation are denied. The second is that, to someone who has accepted this simple division, the conviction of his own rightness is overpowering, and as a result he becomes priggish and self-righteous.

—David Daiches, "Politics and the Literary Imagination," 1971

WHEN THESE WORDS WERE written, the political polarization that has become a cliché of American life in the third decade of the twenty-first century was in its infancy. The "vast Right-wing" conspiracy that Hillary Clinton named in the late 1990s, and which has rightly been credited with fostering so much of this polarization, was just starting to take shape. Kevin Phillips developed his Southern Strategy that viciously stoked animosity between Blacks and Whites in the American South in 1970, Lewis Powell's well-known memo to the U.S. Chamber of Commerce calling for the militant defense of American business against Leftist agitators was written in 1971, the Heritage Foundation was established in 1973, and the radical Right staged their takeover of the NRA in 1977. During this same time, and continuing throughout subsequent decades, this network of conservative thinkers, activists, and politicians turned to political consultant Arthur Finkelstein, who created some of the nastiest and most effective political ads of the late twentieth century on behalf of Republicans and conservatives. Our historical record has begun to reflect some of this conservative activism in the last few decades.[1]

But stories of how political and social polarization developed over the last fifty years are incomplete if they don't consider the effect of Leftist academic radicals on this phenomenon. For one, during the course of researching this book, I began to wonder to what extent the academic Left chronicled in this book is *the* American Left of the post-Vietnam era. Answering such a question is beyond the scope of this book and my expertise, but if there is any extent to which this is true, I wonder how much the success of the Right is owed to the Left's abandoning the public sphere in favor of an ostensibly private one in colleges and universities. Second, the reliance on *ad hominem* attacks by Leftist academic radicals, just briefly mentioned in this manuscript, deserves further scrutiny. A full expository treatment of this phenomenon is also beyond the scope of this book but does deserve exploration. Such an argumentative approach is not, to put it mildly, a strategy of sweet talk that Western rhetoric has counseled and practiced in winning over an opponent for more than two millennia. The use of this argumentative strategy is no doubt, at least in part, the collateral damage of accepting so fully that the personal, and so much else, is political. Third, the multipronged effort to fundamentally upend the epistemological bases of the humanities has not helped Americans to grow more united with the greater recognition of diversity we have achieved in the last fifty years. Fine artists like those included in the *Liberations* volume who sought to radically revise our aesthetic and perceptive experiences undermined an aesthetic humanities. At the same time, cultural theorists whose fundamental goal was to defeat liberal humanism by revealing it as a capitalist prop undermined civic humanities. The epistemological basis of humanistic study was also perhaps weakened by a retreat away from goals of unity and collective experience and into the private and personal. An example of this would be the words of Carolyn Lougee, the Stanford faculty member and administrator discussed in chapter 3 who was so instrumental in ushering in changes to the Western culture program at Stanford. Lougee suggested that the only way general education curricula would include minorities—in her case, women—was if the humanities were redefined. She argued that the humanities must abandon their "maleness"—exemplified by a focus on public life, excellence in an artistic genre, and promoting universality among people—and instead try to establish actual humanistic ends, understood as knowledge that is inclusive of the cultural productions of women and non-Whites. This involves "[freeing] the humanities from the ideal of public life, disciplinary excellence, and human commonality" and focusing instead on "the fragment recorded in private, unknown to contemporaries, perhaps little known to posterity, without traceable influence and therefore part of history, though not of heritage." Both reorienting the epistemological basis of humanistic study and making sure that minorities were represented in educational curricula required, according to Lougee, developing general education courses that "are not bound to the ideals of the public, the genres, and the melting pot."[2]

Overly broad categories like "male"—or, for that matter, women, Black, White, Native American, Asian, differently abled, homosexual, or genderqueer—reduce an opponent into a straw man that, of course, cannot meet the criticisms leveled at it. It is a reliance on an essentialism that was in other places (for example, in feminist theory) anathema to the academic Left. It was on such a basis that Bill Chace, one vocal critic of the proposed changes to the WC program at Stanford, based his concerns. Chace wrote a letter to Carolyn Lougee in her capacity as an associate dean at Stanford in July 1986. In this letter, Chace wrote of his concerns that calls for review of the WC program were based on misapprehensions of the program's guiding assumptions. Those assumptions, created in 1980, were "instrumental" and not "value laden." By this Chace meant that "the faculty took no general position on the question of whether the works and ideas to be studied [in the WC program] were 'Right,' or 'good,' or 'morally improving.'" The faculty believed the chosen works to be "inescapable" because they had proven "over long historical time to be fundamentally important to: an understanding of crucial events—and their consequences—in a vast geographical area extending from the Mediterranean basin to North America over the last 2500 years; an understanding of the basic forms of discourse for the great mass of people in the West for centuries; and an understanding of how the West had, in various terms, been arguing with itself for just as long a time." Chace further lamented the moral criticisms being made of the program, referring to the "most forceful negative argument at least in print in the Stanford Community," an essay published by a student named David Troutt. Chace recalled Troutt's argument that "the [WC] requirement gives a 'dangerously mythological vision of Western culture,' one that is 'narrow' and 'ethnocentric,' one, moreover, that implies that 'the writings, theories, and critiques, of only the upper-class, West European (and Greek) Caucasian males' are 'the basic reality of the West.'" Troutt further argued, according to Chace, that "Western culture, as it stands, is not just racist education, it is the education of racists." Chace was troubled by Troutt's broad claims made without reference to "specific writings." He further found that when he reflected "on the works and writers I have taught over the years in the spring quarter [of the WC program], and when I focus directly on the 'required texts' in that course, I come to the ironic conclusion that, instead of serving to legitimate the status quo of the West or to reinforce the racist or sexist structures surrounding us, those texts do precisely the opposite."[3]

There is a fundamental and perhaps irreconcilable conflict here, one that illuminates the necessary differences between activism and education. Activism often needs big, overly general, reductive concepts, such as those Troutt used, to inspire people to join a movement toward change they might otherwise be unaware of or loath to join. Education, if it is to be good and effective, needs just the opposite— the slow appreciation of the great complexity of the human and natural worlds and instruction in how to navigate such complexity. The reductive quality of broad categories such as those mentioned above fosters a simplicity and dehumanization that lays the ground for the political polarization we live with. All we often need to know about someone is their "brand"—voted for Trump or not, free-marketer or socialist, liberal or conservative. Once we have established any of those points, we can safely reject the entire person. We decide we don't have to understand them and that therefore they can be dismissed—or worse—before the conditions that make understanding between people possible have even been established. The movement away from a humanistic study that values unity and/or commonality across differences, paired with institutions of higher learning accepting and thus conferring the cultural capital that comes with university study on broad, reductive, dehumanizing categories of criticism, establishes a public attitude that fosters the social, political, and cultural conditions for the political polarization we live with today.

We used to, not so long ago, look to the humanities as practiced in American institutions of higher learning to overcome the possibility of such political polarization; there was a sort of unity in diversity that was a part of the humanistic conception Carolyn Lougee sought but that has been vexed in academic environments by the tribalism, reductionism, and consequent dehumanization that seems to arise inherently from identity politics. As it happens, we are in a particularly fortuitous time to return to the idea of "unity in diversity" that could start to heal some of our national wounds. Right now, concerns about the humanities going extinct are being addressed by reconsidering approaches to general education. Recently, the Teagle Foundation partnered with the National Endowment for the Humanities (NEH) on an initiative to "revitalize the role of the humanities in general education." The Teagle Foundation points to a program developed at Purdue called the Cornerstone Integrated Liberal Arts (CILA). CILA is a program where students earn a certificate having completed a two-course sequence in their first year called "Transformative Texts" and then taking other courses in "thematically organized clusters of courses that compliment [*sic*] the technical course load typically required of STEM and other preprofessional majors." In "Transformative Texts," students are mentored by a tenured or tenure-track faculty member, and together they work through readings at least half of which "are drawn from a faculty created and continually revised list of roughly 200 major works." This list fosters a "commonality" between students that "helps create a sense of belonging and intellectual community for students while also allowing faculty the freedom to design syllabi aligned with their own interests."[4]

This idea about intellectual community or a common intellectual experience is one that has bedeviled general education in higher education for 150 years since Charles Eliot instituted the elective model of education at Harvard in the nineteenth century. With this system, Eliot created a perennial problem in American higher education, and we have not been able to develop a model of successful, common general education almost anywhere, if the frequency of program revision at colleges and universities is any indication. There are several reasons for this. First, the focus of professors has increasingly become their academic specialties and subspecialties. This leaves little room for thinking about, let alone teaching, general courses. Additionally, this tendency toward specialization conferred a degree of freedom on

professors that made any suggestion of developing a common curriculum all teachers would teach the basis for a complaint of violating
academic freedom. The possibility of such complaints almost always
render discussions of common education dead on arrival. Moreover,
there has been an educational problem: most general education programs that did achieve commonality just weren't very good. This was
because in the twentieth century, the idea of common general education was often tethered to the idea of "Great Books." Since the 1920s,
many instructors tried to develop common general education programs based on the notion that had initially developed in the first
decade of the twentieth century out of Charles Eliot's "five foot
shelf." First published in 1909, the five-foot shelf was a collection of
books he put together to give a university education to those who had
not gone to a university; it was said that fifteen minutes of reading
in this collection a day would turn the reader into a liberally educated American. Then, in midcentury, Mortimer Adler worked with
Encyclopedia Britannica to develop a somewhat similar collection of
books that was literally titled the "Great Books." However, focus on
a book, per se, makes little pedagogical sense. This focus on a book
instead of on, say, particular questions, ideas, or themes created educational programs that were fragmented, contingent, and ultimately
incoherent because of the failure to draw explicit connections across
books or to choose books that had some sort of natural connection
among them. Adler's Great Books were first published in 1950; only
twenty years later, the intellectual revolution chronicled in this book
began, rendering Adler's effort worse than obsolete in a short period
of time.

The idea of a common intellectual experience for students is one
that is stressed in all the programs funded by the Teagle Foundation
that I reviewed. For example, American University has a program
called "The Examined Life," a seminar in the first year of students'
study. This seminar creates a "common intellectual experience" across
sections by sharing a syllabus developed by faculty working together
and which focuses on "transformative texts" like Plato's *Apology*, *The
Confessions* by Augustine, *Frankenstein* by Mary Shelley, and *The Narrative of the Life of Frederick Douglass, an American Slave*. Similarly, a
two-year college, SUNY Onondaga, developed a program required

for first-year liberal arts students. This experience is considered a "student success course" that "orients new students to the institution and helps them cultivate the skills needed to be successful in college while also using core texts to create a common intellectual experience and a sense of belonging on campus." These eighty "core texts" are reconsidered yearly by faculty and include titles like Virginia Woolf's *To the Lighthouse* and Homer's *Odyssey*. In addition to this first-year program, SUNY Onondaga developed a pathway called "Enduring Questions," which "allows students to complete at least 12 credits of required general education courses that draw on core humanities texts." The University of Nevada–Las Vegas (UNLV) developed a "Great Works Academic Certificate." Attaining the certificate involves taking a "a four course sequence" in the so-called Great Works. After that, students can elect to take a pathway that involves two more courses in the Great Works. UNLV also developed a minor that can be earned with "six credits of elective courses that emphasize transformative texts" in addition to the certificate and pathways courses. These three series of courses are "stackable," which means that students can "meet most of their general education requirements through coursework in the humanities."[5]

In spite of the failure to establish coherent, effective, and common general education programs in all of the twentieth century, it is clear that the time to try again is now. For one, there is already an effort toward this end underway in the partnership between the NEH and Teagle. Second, the intellectual and pedagogical revolution chronicled in this book has produced a vast body of scholarly work that makes our history truer and fairer. Put differently, we now have the tools to develop programs that resist falling victim to accusations of sexism, racism, and/or exclusion because we now have, much more than in the 1980s, materials that can make such programs broad and inclusive. Third, right now, general education in many places is plagued by criticisms of bloat and inefficiency. General education requirements often take up as much as one-third of a student's program of study and are sometimes said to serve professors' job security more than students' education. This is because disciplines will use general education as a place to improve their flagging numbers of majors, thereby making an unpopular program look more essential than it might truly be. Higher education is likely going to go through massive changes in the twenty-first century, due to demographics, technology, runaway costs, consolidation and closure of schools, and experimentation in different possibilities for degree completion. Now more than ever we need informed citizens skilled in critical thinking and civic participation, making this an ideal time to radically rethink how we have heretofore delivered such training. Developing ideas about how to create coherent, civically focused, and efficient general education is going to be possibly the winningest strategy for a brutally competitive educational landscape.

Further, the development of such programs will naturally lead to conversations about the shape and material (in)equality of the professoriat. For example, perhaps it no longer makes sense to materially reward deep expertise, to the extent that we have, in the majority of colleges and universities in the United States. We certainly need deep expertise, and it undoubtedly deserves to be materially supported, but the civic and critical education of students is equally, if not more, important, and we must examine and improve how we are materially recognizing that need. Such efforts will almost certainly require the partnership of universities, private foundations, and/or government funding sources as the Teagle/NEH partnership shows. Similar partnerships have existed for more than eighty years; the development of the *Redbook* at Harvard in the 1940s, the definitive document on general education in the mid-twentieth century discussed in chapter 3, was funded by the State Department. Harvard, of course, doesn't need such support these days, but more such partnerships at some of our land-grant or regional comprehensive schools will likely achieve pedagogical and institutional innovations we desperately need but that have eluded us for 150 years.

NOTES

INTRODUCTION

1. Rorty, *Achieving Our Country*, 90; emphasis added.
2. Fukuyama, *Identity*, 40, 115–18.
3. Appiah, *The Lies That Bind*, 167.
4. Lilla, *The Once and Future Liberal*, 87, 89.
5. To start, see Mason, *Uncivil Agreement*; Lukianoff and Haidt, *The Coddling of the American Mind*; and Campbell and Manning, *The Rise of Victimhood Culture*.
6. Donnellan, "The Criterion of the Least Dangerous Assumption."
7. Crenshaw et al., *Critical Race Theory*.

CHAPTER I
CURRICULAR ACTIVISM ON CAMPUS, 1966–1971

1. Spring, "Education and Progressivism," 54–55.
2. The word "radical" is so easily hurled in invective on the Right and the Left these days that I believe it has lost its meaning. Thus, I wish to define what I mean in this book when I say "radical." The *Oxford English Dictionary* offers two meanings that are germane to my project here: (a) "change or action that goes to the root or origin of something, that touches on or effects what is essential and fundamental, and that is thorough or far-reaching"; (b) "in politics advocating thorough or far reaching political or social reform; representing or supporting an extreme section of a political party." Of course, radicalism per se belongs to both the Right and the Left. We could say at this point in time that the Right has achieved over the last forty years radical—in the sense just defined—*economic* reform with the implementation of free-market theories and the Left has achieved radical cultural reform in the degree to which nonbinary gender is visible and increasingly acceptable in our society.
3. Lasch, *The New Radicalism in America*, ix.
4. Brick, *The Age of Contradiction*, 7, 13.
5. Livingston, *The World Turned Inside Out*, 23, 25.
6. Jacobs and Landau, *The New Radicals*, 4.
7. Brick, *The Age of Contradiction*, 17.

8. Gitlin, *The Sixties*, 2–3.

9. Teodori, *The New Left*, 171–72; emphasis added.

10. Isserman, *If I Had a Hammer*, 209–15.

11. Buhle, *Marxism in the United States*, 227; Marcuse, *Eros and Civilization;* Horkheimer and Adorno, *Dialectic of Enlightenment.*

12. Students for a Democratic Society, "Radical Education Project," 1, 3–4.

13. Students for a Democratic Society, "Radical Education Project," 13.

14. Students for a Democratic Society, "Radical Education Project," 16–17.

15. *Radicals in the Professions*, 1.

16. *Radicals in the Professions*, 6.

17. Krause, "What's Left of the New Left?" 17.

18. Rothenberg and Rothenberg, NUC Newsletter."

19. Krause, "What's Left of the New Left?" 17, 18.

20. Pincus and Ehrlich, "The New University Conference."

21. Roszak, ed., *The Dissenting Academy*, back flap.

22. Theodore Roszak, preface, in Roszak, ed., *The Dissenting Academy*, vii.

23. Roszak, "On Academic Delinquency," 7.

24. Kampf, "The Scandal of Literary Scholarship," 60.

25. Rosen, "Keynes without Gadflies."

26. Lynd, "Historical Past and Existential Present," 102.

27. Windmiller, "The New American Mandarins."

28. Hassan, ed., *Liberations.*

29. Ihab Hassan, preface, in Hassan, ed., *Liberations*, xi.

30. Stern, "The Mysterious New Novel," 30, 32.

31. Wolff, "Understanding the Revolution," 43, 45, 48.

32. White, "The Culture of Criticism," 69.

33. Poirier, "Rock of Ages," 134, 144.

34. Miller, "The 'Classic' American Writers and the Radicalized Curriculum," 566.

35. Purves, "Life, Death, and the Humanities," 560, 561, 562, 564.

36. Franklin, "The Teaching of Literature in the Highest Academies of the Empire," 549, 551, 553.

37. Rogers, "The Black Campus Movement," 22–25, 33.

38. Hare, "Questions and Answers about Black Studies," 727, 728.

39. Hare, "Questions and Answers about Black Studies," 731, 732, 733–34.

40. Spratlen, "Ethnic Studies," 163.

41. Spratlen, "Ethnic Studies," 166.

42. Banks, "Imperatives in Ethnic Minority Education," 266–67.

43. Jacobson, *Roots Too*, 19.

44. Krug, "White Ethnic Studies," 322, 323.

45. San Diego State University, "Women's Studies @ SDSU."

46. Seamas, "55 Campuses Now Offering Courses in Women's Studies," 46.

47. Grahl et al., "Women's Studies," 109, 112–14.

CHAPTER 2
IDENTITY, POLITICS, AND IDENTITY POLITICS

1. Jacobs and Landau, *The New Radicals*, 4.

2. Friedan, *The Feminine Mystique.*

3. Izenberg, *Identity*, 144.
4. Izenberg, *Identity*, 129.
5. Erikson, "The Problem of Ego Identity," 56, 57.
6. Erikson, *Young Man Luther,* 22, 41.
7. Erikson, "The Problem of Ego Identity," 119.
8. Friedan, *The Feminine Mystique*, 69.
9. Millett, *Sexual Politics*, 23, 24.
10. Sampson, *The Psychology of Power*, 34, 185, 16.
11. Sampson, *The Psychology of Power*, 1, 2.
12. Horkheimer, "Materialism and Morality," 103, 106–7, 117, 116, 118.
13. Wallen, "Criticism as Displacement"; Bulson, "Tripping His Brains Out."
14. Foucault, *Power Knowledge*, 39.
15. Said, *Orientalism*, 3.
16. Jameson, *Marxism and Form 20th-Century Dialectical Theories of Literature*; Eagleton, *Myths of Power;* Eagleton, *Literary Theory*.
17. Berman, "Introduction," 7, 8–9.
18. Guillory, *Cultural Capital*, 176, 203.
19. Cunningham, "Theory, What Theory?" 27.
20. Cusset, *French Theory*, xi.
21. Redfield, *Theory at Yale*, 22.
22. Eagleton, *Literary Theory*, 194, 200.
23. Eagleton, *Literary Theory*, 209, 210, 211.
24. Lentricchia, *Criticism and Social Change*, 6, 2.
25. Lentricchia, *Criticism and Social Change*, 8, 7, 11.
26. Izenberg, *Identity,* 175.
27. Combahee River Collective, "A Black Feminist Statement," 16.
28. Rawls, *A Theory of Justice*, 4.
29. Rawls, *A Theory of Justice*, 11.
30. Foucault, *The History of Sexuality*, 10, 11, 23–24, 25.
31. Izenberg, *Identity*, 302–3.
32. Cixous, "The Laugh of the Medusa," 877, 878, 886.
33. Irigaray, *This Sex Which Is Not One*, 24.
34. McIntosh, "The Homosexual Role," 182, 183, 184, 185.
35. Radicalesbians, "The Woman Identified Woman," 1.
36. Firestone, *The Dialectic of Sex,* 7, 15, 31.
37. Firestone, *The Dialectic of Sex,* 36, 188.
38. Lorde, *Uses of the Erotic*, 54, 55, 59.
39. hooks, *Ain't I a Woman*, 15, 7, 8–9.
40. Rich, "Compulsory Heterosexuality and Lesbian Existence," 632.
41. Cherríe Moraga and Gloria Anzaldúa, "Children Passing in the Streets," and "Entering the Lives of Others," both in Moraga and Anzaldúa, *This Bridge Called My Back*, 3, 19.
42. Cherríe Moraga, "La Guera," in Moraga and Anzaldúa, *This Bridge Called My Back*, 23, 24–25.
43. Fanon, *Black Skin, White Masks*, 14, 2, 70, 75.
44. Frye, *The Politics of Reality*, 155, 8, 13, 38.
45. Frye, *The Politics of Reality*, 114, 126.
46. Pateman, *The Sexual Contract*, 102.
47. Phelan, *Identity Politics*, 4, 3.

48. Phelan, *Identity Politics*, 59, 60, 62.

49. Phelan, *Identity Politics*, 63, 69, 71, 73, 76.

50. "120 Years of American Education," 83.

CHAPTER 3
THE CANON WARS AND IDENTITY POLITICS AT STANFORD

1. Bernstein, "Stanford Is Likely to Alter Western Culture Program."

2. Barchas, "Stanford Would Toss Intellectual Heritage to the Winds."

3. Bowen, Attinger, and Pelter, "Education."

4. Vobeja, "Bennett Assails New Stanford Program."

5. Krauthammer, "A Battle Lost at Stanford."

6. Livingston, *The World Turned Inside Out*, 51.

7. Hart, "The Mission of a University."

8. Kirk, "Redoubts of Liberal Education."

9. Sanoff, "Universities Are Turning Out Highly Skilled Barbarians."

10. Griffin, "Panic among the Philistines," August 1981, 42, 50.

11. Jay, "Campus Specialties."

12. Yardley, "Old Words in Woolf's Clothing."

13. Bate, "The Crisis in English Studies," 47, 51, 52.

14. Fish, "Profession Despise Thyself," 353, 354.

15. Bate, "To the Editor of *Critical Inquiry.*"

16. Moglen, "Erosion in the Humanities," 1, 2.

17. Lardner, "War of the Words."

18. Cohen, "There Is Life after the Humanities," 34.

19. Pritchard, "Kind to the Dead, Hard on the Living."

20. "Princeton Fostering Women's Studies."

21. Neusner, "Ethnic Studies, Campus Ghettos," 42, 44.

22. Carnegie Commission on Higher Education, *Reform on Campus*, 23.

23. Butts and Cremin, *A History of Education in American Culture*, 447, 509, 597.

24. Butts and Cremin, *A History of Education in American Culture*, 60.

25. The Committee on the Objectives of a General Education in a Free Society, *General Education in a Free Society*, 229.

26. Engel, "Harvard's Soft Core," 43, 44.

27. Sawhill, "Higher Education in the 1980s," 425, 428.

28. Ryan, "Doldrums in the Ivies."

29. Boyd and Levine, "A Quest for Common Learning."

30. "Legislative History of the Western Culture Program."

31. Committee on Undergraduate Studies, "Recommendation for a Requirement in Western Culture."

32. Hutchinson, "Western Culture Pilot Program."

33. Committee on Undergraduate Studies, "Recommendations on Distribution Requirements."

34. Committee on Undergraduate Studies, "Recommendations on Distribution Requirements."

35. Lougee, "Women, History, and the Humanities," 4.

36. Lougee, "Women, History, and the Humanities," 4–5.
37. Lougee, "Women, History, and the Humanities," 5, 6.
38. Stern, "The Mysterious New Novel."
39. Ukweli and African History Committee of the Black Student Union, "Western Culture Courses Found Lacking."
40. Subcommittee on Gender and Minorities, "None."
41. Giraud, "Widen Western Culture."
42. Giraud, "Widen Western Culture."
43. Green, "Western Culture Is Racist."
44. Black Student Union, Untitled document, April 23, 1986.
45. Katz, Untitled document, November 5, 1986.
46. Black Student Union, "Endorsers of Proposed Spring Quarter Course."
47. Wynter, "A Preliminary Proposal for an Alternative to the Present Core Curriculum Requirements," 3.
48. Carson, "Proposal for a New Western Culture Track."
49. Paik, "BSU Renews Call for World Studies."
50. ASSU Council of Presidents-Elect, Untitled document, May 14, 1986.
51. Lougee, "Attend Western Culture Discussion."
52. Walsh and Beyers, "For Observer Only, Add to Western Culture Story."
53. Riggs, "Course Option OK'd by CUS."
54. Yuh, "C-US Suggests Assessment of Freshman Core."
55. Anderson, "Western Culture Does Not Oppress."
56. Cohn, "Those in Power Permit Heritage to 'Go to the Dogs.'"
57. Rebholz, Untitled document, June 17, 1986.
58. Mahoney, "TF Draft."
59. Sheehan, Untitled document, June 20, 1986.
60. Collier and Janagisako, Untitled document, July 21, 1986.
61. Rosse, "Charge to the Task Force on the Area 1 Requirement."
62. "Students' Charge to the Western Culture Task Force."
63. Black Student Union, Untitled document, September 1986.
64. Seaver, Untitled document, December 5, 1986.
65. Perry, "Notes on Area 1 Requirement."
66. "Introduction: When I Hear the Word 'Culture' I Reach for My Gun," 9.
67. Carson, "Course Title: Critical Studies of Values and Ideas."
68. McCall, Letter to Paul Seaver, February 11, 1987.
69. Seaver, Letter to Marsh McCall, February 14, 1987.
70. Seaver, "Proposed Legislation for Area One Requirement."
71. Seligman, "Draft Area One Requirement."
72. Harvey, "Response to Task Force Proposal."
73. Rebholz, Untitled document, April 20, 1987.
74. Perloff, Untitled document, April 16, 1987.
75. Gelpi, Untitled document, April 15, 1987.
76. Wessells, "Response to Your Solicitation."
77. Wynter, Untitled document, April 20, 1987.
78. Stanford American Indian Organization, Untitled document, April 20, 1987.
79. Robinson, Untitled document, April 20, 1987.
80. Seaver and Necochea, "Proposed Changes and Additions."

81. King, Untitled document, October 30, 1987.
82. Committee on Undergraduate Studies, Untitled document, November 16, 1987.
83. Chace et al., "Area One Requirement Proposed Legislation."
84. Bratman and Lindenberger, "To Be Proposed as Friendly Amendments to SenD#3229."
85. Carson, "Suggested Revision of CUS Proposal."
86. Robinson, "A Proposed Compromise on CIV Legislation."
87. Robinson, "A Proposed Compromise on CIV Legislation."
88. Feldman, "Proposed Amendments."
89. Smith, "Humanities Proposal the Latest in a Long Conflict."
90. Stanford Faculty, "The Study of Undergraduate Education at Stanford University."
91. Watkins, "Farewell to IHUM."
92. "The Case for a Western Civilization Requirement at Stanford."
93. From the Community, "The White Civ's Burden," 1.
94. From the Community, "A Response to the Review's Western Civilization Petition," 3.
95. Contreras, "Humanities Core Implemented," 1.
96. Rezvani, "Stanford Core."
97. Basali, "New First Year Requirement to Debut Next Fall."
98. Edelstein, "Enough with the Culture Wars."

CHAPTER 4
THE ESCALATING CANON WARS AND RACISM AND SEXISM AT THE UNIVERSITY OF TEXAS, AUSTIN

1. Bloom, *The Closing of the American Mind.*
2. Kimball, *Tenured Radicals;* D'Souza, *Illiberal Education;* Bernstein, *Dictatorship of Virtue.*
3. Rorty, *Achieving Our Country*, 83.
4. Bloom, *The Closing of the American Mind*, 25–43, 40, 41 (quotations).
5. Bloom, *The Closing of the American Mind*, 141–56, 217–26, 34, 227, 244–45.
6. Moss, "UT English Classes Changed to Study Civil Rights."
7. Gribben, "Syllabus Would Cloud UT's 306."
8. Gribben, "Letter to the Editor."
9. "A Civil Rights Theme for a Writing Course."
10. Moss, "UT Postpones Plans to Alter English Class."
11. Duban, "A Modest Proposal."
12. Broadkey and Slatin, "Proposed Syllabus Would Enhance 306 Experience."
13. Gribben, "Syllabus Would Cloud UT's 306."
14. Hairston, "Required Courses Should Not Focus on Charged Issues."
15. Mangan, "Entire Writing-Course Panel Quits at U. of Texas."
16. Mangan, "U. of Texas Postpones Writing Course."
17. Mangan, "Entire Writing-Course Panel Quits at U. of Texas."
18. Phillip, "UT English Professor Heading to Denton."
19. Kimball, *Tenured Radicals*, liii.

20. D'Souza, *Illiberal Education*, 13.
21. Yardley, "On Dasher, On Dancer, To Albania."
22. "Campus Life: Massachusetts."
23. Weinraub, "The Book Wars."
24. Berman, *Debating P.C.*
25. Berube, "Public Image Limited," 142.
26. Said, "The Politics of Knowledge," 174–75.
27. Ravitch, "Multiculturalism," 276–77.
28. Asante, "Multiculturalism," 304.
29. Bernstein, *Dictatorship of Virtue*, 38.

CONCLUSION

1. See, for example, Continetti, *The Right*; Lombardo, *Blue Collar Conservativism*; Belew, *Bring the War Home:*; and Perlstein *Reaganland; Nixonland; The Invisible Bridge;* and *Before the Storm.*
2. Lougee, "Women, History, and the Humanities," 6.
3. Chace, "Stanford University Memorandum," June 14, 1986, 2, 3, 4.
4. "The Teagle Foundation—Cornerstone."
5. Bezbatchenko and Pazich, "General Education and the Humanities."

BIBLIOGRAPHY

Adler, J., and M. Starr. "Taking Offense." *Newsweek*, December 1990, 48.

American Indian Community. Untitled document. April 20, 1987. Box 7, folders 1–3, CIV/Area 1, Paul S. Seaver Papers, Stanford University Archives, Palo Alto, CA.

Anderson, Nicholas. "Western Culture Does Not Oppress." May 1986. Box 6, folder 1, series 3, CIV/Area 1, Paul S. Seaver Papers, Stanford University Archives, Palo Alto, CA.

Appiah, Kwame Anthony. *The Lies That Bind: Rethinking Identity*. New York: Liveright, 2018.

Area 1 Task Force. "Proposed Legislation." December 7, 1987. Box 7, folders 4–5, CIV/Area 1, Paul S. Seaver Papers, Stanford University Archives, Palo Alto, CA.

Asante, Molefi Kete. "Multiculturalism: An Exchange." In *Debating P.C.: The Controversy over Political Correctness on College Campuses*, edited by Paul Berman, 299–311. New York: Dell, 1992.

Associated Students of Stanford University (ASSU) Council of Presidents-Elect. Untitled document. May 14, 1986. Box 6, folder 1, series 3, CIV/Area 1, Paul S. Seaver Papers, Stanford University Archives, Palo Alto, CA.

Banks, James A. "Imperatives in Ethnic Minority Education." *Phi Delta Kappan* 53, no. 5 (1972): 266–69.

Barchas, Isaac. "Stanford Would Toss Intellectual Heritage to the Winds." *Wall Street Journal*, January 21, 1988.

Basali, Hannah. "New First Year Requirement to Debut Next Fall." *Stanford Daily*, April 1, 2021.

Bate, W. Jackson. "The Crisis in English Studies." *Harvard Magazine*, October 1982, 46–53.

———. "To the Editor of *Critical Inquiry*." *Critical Inquiry* 10, no 2 (December 1983): 365–70.

"Behind the Push to Revive the Liberal Arts in US Colleges." *US News and World Report*, May 1977.

Belew, Kathleen. *Bring the War Home: The White Power Movement and Military America*. Cambridge, MA: Harvard University Press, 2019.

Berman, Paul, ed. *Debating P.C.: The Controversy over Political Correctness on College Campuses*. New York: Dell, 1992.

———. "Introduction: The Debate and Its Origins." In *Debating P.C.: The Controversy over Political Correctness on College Campuses*, edited by Paul Berman, 1–26. New York: Dell, 1992.

Bernstein, Richard. *Dictatorship of Virtue: How the Battle Over Multiculturalism Is Reshaping Our Schools, Our Country, and Our Lives*. 1994; reprint New York: Vintage Books, 1995.

———. "Stanford Is Likely to Alter Western Culture Program." *New York Times*, January 19, 1988.

Berube, Michael. "Public Image Limited: Political Correctness and the Media's Big Lie." In *Debating P.C.: The Controversy over Political Correctness on College Campuses*, edited by Paul Berman, 124–49. New York: Dell, 1992.

Bezbatchenko, Annie W., and Loni Bordoloi Pazich. "General Education and the Humanities." American Association of Colleges and Universities, January 14, 2022. https://www.aacu.org.

Black Student Union. "Endorsers of Proposed Spring Quarter Course." May 19, 1986. Box 6, folder 1, series 3, CIV/Area 1, Paul S. Seaver Papers, Stanford University Archives, Palo Alto, CA.

———. Untitled document. April 23, 1986. Box 6, folder 1, series 3, CIV/Area 1, Paul S. Seaver Papers, Stanford University Archives, Palo Alto, CA.

———. Untitled document. September 1986. Box 6, folder 1, series 3, CIV/Area 1, Paul S. Seaver Papers, Stanford University Archives, Palo Alto, CA.

Bloom, Allan. *The Closing of the American Mind: How Higher Education Has Failed Democracy and Impoverished the Souls of Today's Students*. New York: Simon and Schuster, 1987.

Bowen, Ezra, Joelle Attinger, and Charles Pelter. "Education: The Canons under Fire." *Time*, April 11, 1988, 66.

Boyd, Ernest, and Arthur Levine. "A Quest for Common Learning." *Change: The Magazine of Higher Learning* 13, no. 3 (April 1981): 28–35.

Bratman, M. E., and H. S. Lindenberger. "To Be Proposed as Friendly Amendments to SenD#3229." February 11, 1988. Box 7, folder 6, CIV/Area 1, Paul S. Seaver Papers, Stanford University Archives, Palo Alto, CA.

Brick, Howard. *The Age of Contradiction: American Thought and Culture in the 1960s*. New York: Twayne, 1998.

Broadkey, Linda, and John Slatin. "Proposed Syllabus Would Enhance 306 Experience." *Austin [TX] American-Statesman*, September 2, 1990.

Buhle, Paul. *Marxism in the United States: Remapping the History of the American Left.* Brooklyn, NY: Verso, 1991.

Bulson, Eric. "Tripping His Brains Out: When Foucault Took LSD in Death Valley." *Times Literary Supplement,* May 17, 2019.

Butts, R. Freeman, and Lawrence A. Cremin. *A History of Education in American Culture.* New York: Holt, 1953.

Campbell, Bradley, and Jason Manning. *The Rise of Victimhood Culture: Microaggressions, Safe Spaces and the New Culture Wars.* London: Palgrave Macmillan, 2018.

"Campus Life: Massachusetts: Should a Writing Class Teach Social Diversity." *New York Times,* February 3, 1991.

Carnegie Commission on Higher Education. *Reform on Campus: Changing Students, Changing Academics.* New York: McGraw-Hill, 1972.

Carson, Clayborne. "Course Title: Critical Studies of Values and Ideas." N.d. Box 5, folder 2, series 3, CIV/Area 1, Paul S. Seaver Papers, Stanford University Archives, Palo Alto, CA.

———. "Proposal for a New Western Culture Track, 3rd Quarter Course—Western Culture and Its Victims." October 1986. Box 6, folder 1, series 3, CIV/Area 1, Paul S. Seaver Papers, Stanford University Archives, Palo Alto, CA.

———. "Suggested Revision of CUS Proposal." February 11, 1988. Box 7, folder 6, CIV/Area 1, Paul S. Seaver Papers, Stanford University Archives, Palo Alto, CA.

"The Case for a Western Civilization Requirement at Stanford." *Stanford Review,* February 21, 2016.

Chace, William M. "Stanford University Memorandum." June 14, 1986. Box 5, folder 1, series 3, CIV/Area 1, Paul S. Seaver Papers, Stanford University Archives, Palo Alto, CA.

———. "The Western Culture Program." June 16, 1986. Box 5, folder 2, CIV/Area 1, Paul S. Seaver Papers, Stanford University Archives, Palo Alto, CA.

Chace, William M., et al. "Area One Requirement Proposed Legislation." January 11, 1988. Box 7, folder 6, CIV/Area 1, Paul S. Seaver Papers, Stanford University Archives, Palo Alto, CA.

"A Civil Rights Theme for a Writing Course." *New York Times,* June 24, 1990.

Cixous, Hélène. "The Laugh of the Medusa." *Signs* 1, no. 4 (1976): 875–93.

Cohen, J. "There Is Life after the Humanities." *Wall Street Journal,* January 22, 1985.

Cohn, Robert Greer. "Those in Power Permit Heritage to 'Go to the Dogs.'" *Campus Report.* June 4, 1986. Box 6, folder 1, series 3, CIV/Area 1, Paul S. Seaver Papers, Stanford University Archives, Palo Alto, CA.

Collier, Jane F., and Sylvia Janagisako. Untitled document. July 21, 1986. Box 6, folder 1, series 3, CIV/Area 1, Paul S. Seaver Papers, Stanford University Archives, Palo Alto, CA.

Combahee River Collective. "A Black Feminist Statement." In *All the Women Are White, All the Blacks Are Men, but Some of Us Are Brave*, edited by Gloria T Hull, Patricia Bell Scott, and Barbara Smith, 13–22. New York: Feminist Press, 1982.

The Committee on the Objectives of a General Education in a Free Society. *General Education in a Free Society*. Cambridge, MA: Harvard University Press, 1945.

Committee on Undergraduate Studies. "Recommendation for a Requirement in Western Culture." May 17, 1978. Box 5, folder 1, series 3, CIV/Area 1, Paul S. Seaver Papers, Stanford University Archives, Palo Alto, CA.

———. "Recommendations on Distribution Requirements, Including the Proposed Western Culture Requirement." November 28, 1979. Box 5, folder 1, series 3, CIV/Area 1, Paul S. Seaver Papers, Stanford University Archives, Palo Alto, CA.

———. "Report of CUS on Area 1 Legislation Proposed by the Provostial Task Force." Stanford University, January 15, 1988. Box 7, folder 6, CIV/Area 1, Paul S. Seaver Papers, Stanford University Archives, Palo Alto, CA.

———. Untitled document. November 16, 1987. Box 6, folders 4–5, CIV/Area 1, Paul S. Seaver Papers, Stanford University Archives, Palo Alto, CA.

Continetti, Matthew. *The Right: The Hundred Year War for American Conservatism*. New York: Basic Books, 2022.

Contreras, Brian. "Humanities Core Implemented." *Stanford Daily*, October 25, 2016.

Crenshaw, Kimberle Williams, et al. *Critical Race Theory: The Key Writings That Formed the Movement*. New York: New Press, 1996.

Cunningham, Valerie. "Theory, What Theory?" In *Theory's Empire*, edited by Daphne Patai and Will H. Corral, 24–41. New York: Columbia University Press, 2005.

Cusset, François. *French Theory: How Foucault, Derrida, Deleuze, and Co. Transformed the Intellectual Life of the United States*. Minneapolis: University of Minnesota Press, 2008.

Daiches, David. "Politics and the Literary Imagination." In *Liberations: New Essays on the Humanities in Revolution*, edited by Ihab Hassan, 100–116. Middletown, CT: Wesleyan University Press, 1971.

Delbanco, Andrew, and Loni Bordoloi Pazich. "Reviving the Humanities through General Education." *Inside Higher Ed*, October 18, 2021, https://www.insidehighered.com.

Donnellan, Anne M. "The Criterion of the Least Dangerous Assumption."
  Behavioral Disorders 9, no. 2 (1984): 141–50.
D'Souza, Dinesh. *Illiberal Education: The Politics of Race and Sex on Campus.*
  New York: Free Press, 1991.
Duban, James. "A Modest Proposal: Stick to Writing in E306 at UT." *Austin [TX] American-Statesman*, August 26, 1990.
Eagleton, Terry. *Literary Theory: An Introduction.* Hoboken, NJ: Blackwell,
  1983.
———. *Marxism and Literary Criticism.* Oxfordshire, UK: Routledge, 2013.
———. *Myths of Power: A Marxist Study of the Brontës.* London: Palgrave
  Macmillan, 2005.
Edelstein, Dan. "Enough with the Culture Wars." *Inside Higher Ed,* March
  30, 2022, https://www.insidehighered.com.
Engel, Peter. "Harvard's Soft Core." *Washington Monthly,* January 1980.
Erikson, Erik H. "The Problem of Ego Identity." *Journal of the American
  Psychoanalytic Association* 4, no. 1 (1956): 56–121.
———. *Young Man Luther: A Study in Psychoanalysis and History.* New
  York: Norton, 1962.
Fanon, Frantz. *Black Skin, White Masks.* New York: Grove Press, 2008.
Feldman, Gary J. "Proposed Amendments." March 29, 1988. Box 7, folder
  6, CIV/Area 1, Paul S. Seaver Papers, Stanford University Archives,
  Palo Alto, CA.
Firestone, Shulamith. *The Dialectic of Sex: The Case for Feminist Revolution.*
  1970; reprint New York: Farrar, Straus and Giroux, 2003.
Fish, Stanley. "Profession Despise Thyself: Fear and Self-Loathing in Literary Studies." *Critical Inquiry* 10, no. 2 (1983): 349–64.
Foucault, Michael. *The History of Sexuality: An Introduction.* New York:
  Vintage Books, 1990.
———. *Power/Knowledge: Selected Interviews and Other Writings.* New
  York: Random House, 1988.
Franklin, Bruce. "The Teaching of Literature in the Highest Academies of
  the Empire." *College English* 31, no. 6 (1970): 548–57.
Friedan, Betty. *The Feminine Mystique.* New York: Norton, 2010.
From the Community. "A Response to the Review's Western Civilization
  Petition." *Stanford Daily,* February 23, 2016.
———. "The White Civ's Burden." *Stanford Daily,* February 22, 2016.
Frye, Marilyn. *The Politics of Reality: Essays in Feminist Theory.* Feasterville-Trevose, PA: Crossing Press, 1983.
Fukuyama, Francis. *Identity: The Demand for Dignity and the Politics of
  Resentment.* New York: Farrar, Straus, and Giroux, 2018.
Gelpi, Albert. Untitled document. April 15, 1987. Box 7, folders 1–3, CIV/
  Area 1, Paul S. Seaver Papers, Stanford University Archives, Palo
  Alto, CA.

Gilbert, Jay. "E Pluribus Unum." January 8, 1987. Box 6, folder 3, series 3, CIV/Area 1, Paul S. Seaver Papers, Stanford University Archives, Palo Alto, CA.

Giraud, Raymond. "Widen Western Culture." February 9, 1986. Box 6, folder 1, series 3, CIV/Area 1, Paul S. Seaver Papers, Stanford University Archives, Palo Alto, CA.

Gitlin, Todd. *The Sixties: Years of Hope, Days of Rage.* Revised edition. New York: Bantam, 1993.

Grahl, Christine, et al. "Women's Studies: A Case in Point." *Feminist Studies* 1, no. 2 (1972): 109–20.

Green, Joseph. "Western Culture Is Racist." *Stanford Daily*, April 22, 1986. Box 6, folder 1, series 3, CIV/Area 1, Paul S. Seaver Papers, Stanford University Archives, Palo Alto, CA.

Gribben, Alan. "Letter to the Editor." *Austin [TX] American-Statesman*, September 14, 1990.

———. "Syllabus Would Cloud UT's 306." *Austin [TX] American-Statesman*, September 8, 1990.

Griffin, Bryan F. "Panic among the Philistines—The Collapse of the Literary Establishment." *Harper's Magazine*, August 1981, 37–52. https://harpers.org.

———. "Panic among the Philistines—The Literary Vulgarians." *Harper's Magazine*, September 1981, 41–56. https://harpers.org.

Guillory, John. *Cultural Capital: The Problem of Literary Canon Formation.* Chicago: University of Chicago Press, 1995.

Hairston, Maxine. "Required Courses Should Not Focus on Charged Issues." *Chronicle of Higher Education*, January 23, 1991, https://www.chronicle.com.

Hare, Nathan. "Questions and Answers about Black Studies." *Massachusetts Review* 10, no. 4 (1969): 727–36.

Hart, Jeffrey. "The Mission of a University." *National Review*, October 1980, 1188.

Harvey, Van. "Response to Task Force Proposal." April 17, 1987. Box 7, folders 1–3, CIV/Area 1, Paul S. Seaver Papers. Stanford University Archives, Palo Alto, CA.

Hassan, Ihab, ed. *Liberations: New Essays on the Humanities in Revolution.* Middletown, CT: Wesleyan University Press, 1971.

hooks, bell. *Ain't I a Woman: Black Women and Feminism.* 1981; reprint Oxfordshire, UK: Routledge, 2014.

Horkheimer, Max. "Materialism and Morality." *Telos* 21, no. 69 (1986): 85–118.

Horkheimer, Max, and Theodor Adorno. *Dialectic of Enlightenment.* Palo Alto, CA: Stanford University Press, 2007.

Hutchinson, Eric. "Western Culture Pilot Program." May 30, 1978. Box 5, folder 1, series 3, CIV/Area 1, Paul S. Seaver Papers, Stanford University Archives, Palo Alto, CA.

"Introduction: When I Hear the Word 'Culture' I Reach for My Gun." N.d. Box 5, folder 2, series 3, CIV/Area 1, Paul S. Seaver Papers, Stanford University Archives, Palo Alto, CA.

Irigaray, Luce. *This Sex Which Is Not One.* Ithaca, NY: Cornell University Press, 1985.

Isserman, Maurice. *If I Had a Hammer: The Death of the Old Left and the Birth of the New Left.* Urbana-Champaign: University of Illinois Press, 1993.

Izenberg, Gerald. *Identity: The Necessity of a Modern Idea.* Philadelphia: University of Pennsylvania Press, 2016.

Jacobs, Paul, and Saul Landau. *The New Radicals: A Report with Documents.* New York: Random House, 1966.

Jacobson, Matthew Frye. *Roots Too: White Ethnic Revival in Post Civil Rights America.* Cambridge, MA: Harvard University Press, 2006.

Jameson, Fredric. *Marxism and Form: 20th-Century Dialectical Theories of Literature.* Princeton, NJ: Princeton University Press, 1972.

Jay, Peter. "Campus Specialties: A Second Rater's Form of Job Insurance." *Baltimore Sun*, September 5, 1982.

Kampf, Louis. "The Scandal of Literary Scholarship." In *The Dissenting Academy: Essays Criticizing the Teaching of the Humanities in American Universities*, edited by Theodore Roszak, 43–61. London: Penguin Books, 1967.

Katz, Barry. Untitled document. November 5, 1986. Box 5, folder 2, series 3, CIV/Area 1, Paul S. Seaver Papers, Stanford University Archives, Palo Alto, CA.

Kimball, Roger. *Tenured Radicals: How Politics Has Corrupted Our Higher Education.* New York City: Harper and Row, 1990.

King, William F. Untitled document. October 30, 1987. Box 7, folder 5, CIV/Area 1, Paul S. Seaver Papers. Stanford University Archives, Palo Alto, CA.

Kirk, Russell. "Redoubts of Liberal Education." *National Review* 32, no. 15 (July 1980): 907.

Krause, Charles A. "What's Left of the New Left? The New University Conference." *New Republic*, March 1971, 17–18.

Krauthammer, Charles. "A Battle Lost at Stanford." *Washington Post*, April 22, 1988.

Krug, Mark M. "White Ethnic Studies: Prospects and Pitfalls." *Phi Delta Kappan* 53, no. 5 (1972): 322–24.

Lardner, James. "War of the Words." *Washington Post*, March 6, 1983.

Lasch, Christopher. *The New Radicalism in America, 1889–1963: The Intellectual as a Social Type*. New York: Norton & Company, 1997.

"Legislative History of the Western Culture Program." N.d. Box 6, folder 2, series 3, CIV/Area 1, Paul S. Seaver Papers, Stanford University Archives, Palo Alto, CA.

Lentricchia, Frank. *Criticism and Social Change*. 1983; reprint Chicago: University of Chicago Press, 1985.

Lilla, Mark. *The Once and Future Liberal: After Identity Politics*. New York: HarperCollins, 2017.

Livingston, James. *The World Turned Inside Out*. Washington, DC: Rowman and Littlefield, 2010.

Lombardo, Timothy. *Blue Collar Conservatism: Frank Rizzo's Philadelphia and Populist Politics*. Philadelphia: University of Pennsylvania Press, 2021.

Lorde, Audre. *Sister, Outsider*. Feasterville-Trevose, PA: Crossing Press, 2007.

———. *Uses of the Erotic: The Erotic as Power*. Tucson, AZ: Kore Press, 2000.

Lougee, Carolyn. "Attend Western Culture Discussion." N.d. Box 6, folder 1, series 3, CIV/Area 1, Paul S. Seaver Papers, Stanford University Archives, Palo Alto, CA.

———. "Women, History, and the Humanities: An Argument in Favor of the General Studies Curriculum." *Women's Studies Quarterly* 9, no. 1 (1981): 4–7.

Lukianoff, Greg, and Jonathan Haidt. *The Coddling of the American Mind*. New York: Penguin, 2018.

Lynd, Staughton. "Historical Past and Existential Present." In *The Dissenting Academy: Essays Criticizing the Teaching of the Humanities in American Universities*, edited by Theodore Roszak, 92–109. London: Penguin Books, 1967.

Mahoney, Sally. "TF Draft." June 19, 1986. Box 6, folder 1, series 3, CIV/Area 1, Paul S. Seaver Papers, Stanford University Archives, Palo Alto, CA.

Mangan, Katherine. "Entire Writing-Course Panel Quits at U. of Texas." *Chronicle of Higher Education*, February 13, 1991, https://www.chronicle.com.

———. "U. of Texas Postpones Writing Course, Kindles Debate over Role of Outsiders in Academic Policy." *Chronicle of Higher Education*, February 20, 1991, https://www.chronicle.com.

Marcuse, Herbert. *Eros and Civilization: A Philosophical Inquiry into Freud*. Boston: Beacon Press, 1974.

Mason, Lilliana. *Uncivil Agreement: How Politics Became Our Identity*. Chicago: University of Chicago Press, 2018.

McCall, Marsh. Letter to Paul Seaver, February 14, 1987. Box 6, folder 3, and box 7, folders 1–3, series 3, CIV/Area 1, Paul S. Seaver Papers, Stanford University Archives, Palo Alto, CA.

McIntosh, Mary. "The Homosexual Role." *Social Problems* 16, no. 2 (Autumn 1968): 182–92.

Miller, James E. "The 'Classic' American Writers and the Radicalized Curriculum." *College English* 31, no. 6 (1970): 565–70.

Millett, Kate. *Sexual Politics*. 1969; reprint New York: Columbia University Press, 2016.

Moglen, Helene. "Erosion in the Humanities: Blowing the Dust from Our Eyes." *Profession* (1983): 1–6.

Moraga, Cherríe, and Gloria Anzaldúa. *This Bridge Called My Back: Writings by Radical Women of Color*. 4th edition. Albany, NY: SUNY Press, 2015.

Moss, Kirby. "UT English Classes Changed to Study Civil Rights." *Austin [TX] American-Statesman*, May 31, 1990.

———. "UT Postpones Plans to Alter English Class." *Austin [TX] American-Statesman*, July 24, 1990.

Neusner, Jacob. "Ethnic Studies, Campus Ghettos." *National Review*, June 15, 1984, 42–44, 61.

"120 Years of American Education: A Statistical Portrait." National Center for Education Statistics, U.S. Department of Education. January 19, 1993. https://nces.ed.gov.

Paik, Felicia. "BSU Renews Call for World Studies." *Stanford Daily*, April 24, 1986. Box 6, folder 1, series 3, CIV/Area 1, Paul S. Seaver Papers, Stanford University Archives, Palo Alto, CA.

Pateman, Carole. *The Sexual Contract*. 1988; reprint Hoboken, NJ: Wiley, 2018.

Perloff, Marjorie. Untitled document. April 16, 1987. Box 7, folders 1–3, CIV/Area 1, Paul S. Seaver Papers, Stanford University Archives, Palo Alto, CA.

Perlstein, Rick. *Before the Storm: Barry Goldwater and the Unmaking of the American Consensus*. New York: Bold Type, 2009.

———. *The Invisible Bridge: The Fall of Nixon and the Rise of Reagan*. New York: Simon and Schuster, 2015.

———. *Nixonland: The Rise of a President and the Fracturing of America*. New York: Scribners, 2009.

———. *Reaganland: America's Right Turn, 1976–1980*. New York: Simon and Schuster, 2020.

Perry, John. "Notes on Area 1 Requirement." N.d. Box 5, folder 2, series 3, CIV/Area 1, Paul S. Seaver Papers, Stanford University Archives, Palo Alto, CA.

Phelan, Shane. *Identity Politics: Lesbian Feminism and the Limits of Community*. 1989; reprint Philadelphia: Temple University Press, 2010.

Phillip, Brooks A. "UT English Professor Heading to Denton." *Austin [TX] American-Statesman*, May 16, 1992.

Pincus, Fred L., and Howard J. Ehrlich. "The New University Conference: A Study of Former Members." *Critical Sociology* 15, no. 2 (July 1988): 145–47.

Poirier, Richard. "Rock of Ages." In *Liberations: New Essays on the Humanities in Revolution*, edited by Ihab Hassan, 131–46. Middletown, CT: Wesleyan University Press, 1971.

"Princeton Fostering Women's Studies." *New York Times*, June 16, 1985.

Pritchard, William H. "Kind to the Dead, Hard on the Living." *New York Times*, February 24, 1985.

Purves, Alan C. "Life, Death, and the Humanities." *College English* 31, no. 6 (1970): 558–64.

Radicalesbians. "The Woman Identified Woman." In *For Lesbians Only: A Separatist Anthology*, edited by Sarah Lucia Hoagland and Julia Penelope, 17–22. London: Onlywomen Press, 1988.

Radicals in the Professions: Selected Papers. Ann Arbor and Detroit, MI: Radical Education Project, 1967.

Ravitch, Diane. "Multiculturalism: E Pluribus Plures." In *Debating P.C.: The Controversy Over Political Correctness on College Campuses*, edited by Paul Berman, 271–98. New York: Dell, 1992.

Rawls, John. *A Theory of Justice*. Cambridge, MA: Belknap Press of Harvard University Press, 1971.

Rebholz, Ron. Untitled document. June 17, 1986. Box 6, folder 1, series 3, CIV/Area 1, Paul S. Seaver Papers, Stanford University Archives, Palo Alto, CA.

———. Untitled document. April 20, 1987. Box 7, folders 1–3, CIV/Area 1, Paul S. Seaver Papers, Stanford University Archives, Palo Alto, CA.

Redfield, Marc. *Theory at Yale: The Strange Case of Deconstruction in America*. New York: Fordham University Press, 2015.

Rezvani, Leily. "Stanford Core: Faculty Proposes New First-Year Requirement Focused on Civic Education." *Stanford Daily*, September 24, 2019.

Rich, Adrienne. "Compulsory Heterosexuality and Lesbian Existence." *Signs* 5, no. 4 (1980): 631–60.

Riggs, Elaine. "Course Option OK'd by CUS." *Stanford Daily*, June 4, 1986. Box 6, folder 1, series 3, CIV/Area 1, Paul S. Seaver Papers, Stanford University Archives, Palo Alto, CA.

Robinson, Paul. "A Proposed Compromise on CIV Legislation." March 16, 1988. Box 7, folder 6, CIV/Area 1, Paul S. Seaver Papers, Stanford University Archives, Palo Alto, CA.

———. Untitled document. April 20, 1987. Box 7, folders 1–3, CIV/Area 1, Paul S. Seaver Papers, Stanford University Archives, Palo Alto, CA.

Rogers, Ibram H. "The Black Campus Movement and the Institutionalization of Black Studies, 1965–1970." *Journal of African American Studies*
16, no. 1 (March 2012): 21–40.

Rorty, Richard. *Achieving Our Country: Leftist Thought in Twentieth-Century
America.* Cambridge, MA: Harvard University Press, 1998.

Rosen, Sumner M. "Keynes without Gadflies." In *The Dissenting Academy:
Essays Criticizing the Teaching of the Humanities in American Universities,* edited by Theodore Roszak, 62–91. London: Penguin Books, 1967.

Rosse, James N. "Charge to the Task Force on the Area 1 Requirement."
September 29, 1986. Box 6, folder 1, series 3, CIV/Area 1, Paul S.
Seaver Papers, Stanford University Archives, Palo Alto, CA.

Roszak, Theodore, ed. *The Dissenting Academy: Essays Criticizing the Teaching of the Humanities in American Universities.* London: Penguin
Books, 1967.

———. "On Academic Delinquency." In *The Dissenting Academy: Essays
Criticizing the Teaching of the Humanities in American Universities,*
edited by Theodore Roszak, 3–42. London: Penguin Books, 1967.

Rothenberg, Marcia, and Mel Rothenberg. "NUC Newsletter." August
21, 1968. New University Conference, Indiana University Chapter Records, Collection C602, Indiana University Archives,
Bloomington.

Rothenberg, Paula S. *Racism and Sexism: An Integrated Study.* New York: St.
Martin's Press, 1987.

Ryan, Mark B. "Doldrums in the Ivies: A Proposal Restoring Self Knowledge to a Liberal Education." *Change* 12, no. 8 (1980): 32.

Said, Edward. *Orientalism.* New York: Vintage Books, 1979.

———. "The Politics of Knowledge." In *Debating P.C.: The Controversy over
Political Correctness on College Campuses,* edited by Paul Berman,
172–89. New York: Dell, 1992.

Salganik, William A. "A Conversation with Steven Mueller, President of
Johns Hopkins." *Change: The Magazine of Higher Learning* 12, no. 7
(1980): 32–35.

Sampson, Ronald. *The Psychology of Power.* New York: Pantheon Books,
1966.

San Diego State University. "Women's Studies @ SDSU." April 16, 2019.

Sanoff, A. "Universities Are Turning Out Highly Skilled Barbarians." *US
News and World Report,* November 1980.

Sawhill, John. "Higher Education in the 1980s." *Vital Speeches of the Day* 46,
no. 40 (May 1980): 425–30.

Seamas, P. W. "55 Campuses Now Offering Courses in Women's Studies."
Chronicle of Higher Education, 1970.

Seaver, Paul. "Draft for Discussion of Some Elements of a Possible Area
One Requirement." December 5, 1986. Box 5, folder 2, series 3, CIV/

Area 1, Paul S. Seaver Papers, Stanford University Archives, Palo Alto, CA.

———. Letter to Marsh McCall, February 11, 1987. Box 6, folder 3, and box 7, folders 1–3, series 3, CIV/Area 1, Paul S. Seaver Papers, Stanford University Archives, Palo Alto, CA.

———. "Proposed Legislation for Area One Requirement." June 1987. Box 6, folder 3, series 3, CIV/Area 1, Paul S. Seaver Papers, Stanford University Archives, Palo Alto, CA.

———. "Stanford University Office Memorandum." June 15, 1987. Box 6, folder 7, CIV/Area 1, Paul S. Seaver Papers, Stanford University Archives, Palo Alto, CA.

———. Untitled document. December 5, 1986. Box 6, folder 1, series 3, CIV/Area 1, Paul S. Seaver Papers, Stanford University Archives, Palo Alto, CA.

———. Untitled document. February 14, 1987. Box 6, folder 3, series 3, CIV/Area 1, Paul S. Seaver Papers, Stanford University Archives, Palo Alto, CA.

Seaver, Paul, and Fernando de Necochea. "Proposed Changes and Additions." October 29, 1987. Box 7, folder 5, CIV/Area 1, Paul S. Seaver Papers, Stanford University Archives, Palo Alto, CA.

———. "Suggested Revisions of C-US Proposed Legislation." March 8, 1988. Box 7, folder 6, CIV/Area 1, Paul S. Seaver Papers, Stanford University Archives, Palo Alto, CA.

Seligman, A. E. "Draft Area One Requirement." April 17, 1987. Box 7, folders 1–3, CIV/Area 1, Paul S. Seaver Papers, Stanford University Archives, Palo Alto, CA.

Sheehan, James. Untitled document. June 20, 1986. Box 6, folder 1, series 3, CIV/Area 1, Paul S. Seaver Papers, Stanford University Archives, Palo Alto, CA.

Smith, Caleb. "Humanities Proposal the Latest in a Long Conflict." *Stanford Daily*, February 23, 2016.

Spratlen, Thad H. "Ethnic Studies: The Challenge of Subcultural Perspectives in American Higher Education." *Soundings: An Interdisciplinary Journal* 52, no. 2 (1969): 162–71.

Spring, Joel. "Education and Progressivism." *History of Education Quarterly* 10, no. 1 (Spring 1970): 53–71.

Stanford American Indian Organization. Untitled document. April 20, 1987. Box 7, folders 1–3, CIV/Area 1, Paul S. Seaver Papers, Stanford University Archives, Palo Alto, CA.

Stanford Faculty. "The Study of Undergraduate Education at Stanford University." January 2012.

Stern, Daniel. "The Mysterious New Novel." In *Liberations: New Essays on the Humanities in Revolution*, edited by Ihab Hassan, 22–37. Middletown, CT: Wesleyan University Press, 1971.

"Students' Charge to the Western Culture Task Force." August 1986. Box 6, folder 1, series 3, CIV/Area 1, Paul S. Seaver Papers, Stanford University Archives, Palo Alto, CA.

Students for a Democratic Society. "Radical Education Project." 1966.

Subcommittee on Gender and Minorities. "None." June 10, 1985. Box 5, folder 1, series 3, CIV/Area 1, Paul S. Seaver Papers, Stanford University Archives, Palo Alto, CA.

"The Teagle Foundation—Cornerstone: Learning for Living." https://www.teaglefoundation.org.

Teodori, Massimo. *The New Left: A Documentary History.* Indianapolis: Bobbs-Merrill, 1969.

Ukweli, Kusema, and African History Committee of the Black Student Union. "Western Culture Courses Found Lacking." *Campus Report.* April 20, 1983. Box 5, folder 1, series 3, CIV/Area 1, Paul S. Seaver Papers, Stanford University Archives, Palo Alto, CA.

Vobeja, Barbara. "Bennett Assails New Stanford Program." *Washington Post,* April 19, 1988.

Wallen, Jeffrey. "Criticism as Displacement." In *Theory's Empire,* edited by Daphne Patai and Will H Corral, 476–89. New York: Columbia University Press, 2005.

Walsh, Eileen, and Bob Beyers. "For Observer Only, Add to Western Culture Story." N.d. Box 6, folder 1, series 3, CIV/Area 1, Paul S. Seaver Papers, Stanford University Archives, Palo Alto, CA.

Watkins, Marshall. "Farewell to IHUM." *Stanford Daily,* March 9, 2012.

Weinraub, Judith. "The Book Wars: Campuses Split over the New Multicultural Criteria." *Washington Post,* April 7, 1991.

Wessells, Norman K. "Response to Your Solicitation." April 16, 1987. Box 7, folders 1–3, CIV/Area 1, Paul S. Seaver Papers, Stanford University Archives, Palo Alto, CA.

White, Hayden. "The Culture of Criticism." In *Liberations: Essays on the Humanities in Revolution,* edited by Ihab Hassan, 55–69. Middletown, CT: Wesleyan University Press, 1971.

Windmiller, Marshall. "The New American Mandarins." In *The Dissenting Academy: Essays Criticizing the Teaching of the Humanities in American Universities,* edited by Theodore Roszak, 110–34. London: Penguin Books, 1967.

Wolff, Michael. "Understanding the Revolution: The Arena of Victorian Britain." In *Liberations: New Essays on the Humanities in Revolution,* edited by Ihab Hassan, 41–54. Middletown, CT: Wesleyan University Press, 1971.

Wynter, Sylvia. "A Preliminary Proposal for an Alternative to the Present Core Curriculum Requirements." May 1986. Box 6, folder 1, series 3, CIV/Area 1, Paul S. Seaver Papers, Stanford University Archives, Palo Alto, CA.

————. Untitled document. April 20, 1987. Box 7, folders 1–3, CIV/Area 1,
    Paul S. Seaver Papers, Stanford University Archives, Palo Alto, CA.
Yardley, Jonathan. "Old Words in Woolf's Clothing." *Washington Post*,
    November 8, 1982.
————. "On Dasher, on Dancer, to Albania." *Washington Post*, December
    24, 1990.
Yuh, Mary. "C-US Suggests Assessment of Freshman Core." *Stanford
    Daily*, May 22, 1986. Box 6, folder 1, series 3, CIV/Area 1, Paul S.
    Seaver Papers, Stanford University Archives, Palo Alto, CA.

INDEX

ELIZABETH KALBFLEISCH was born in Akron, Ohio, and is currently associate professor of English at Southern Connecticut State University in New Haven, Connecticut. She holds a PhD in rhetoric from the University of Minnesota and has published articles on rhetoric history, theory, pedagogy, and post-secondary academic literacy. She currently lives in Hamden, Connecticut, with her husband and son.